Baking

Real

Bread

Hawthorn Press

Hawthorn Press
Published by Hawthorn Press, Hawthorn House,
1 Lansdown Lane, Stroud, Gloucestershire, GL5 1BJ, UK
Tel: (01453) 757040
Email: info@hawthornpress.com
www.hawthornpress.com

Drawings and cover illustration © Marije Rowling
Cover design and typesetting by Lucy Guenot
Printed by CMP (UK) Ltd.
Printed on environmentally friendly chlorine-free paper sourced from renewable forest stock.

Every effort has been made to trace the ownership of all copyrighted material. If any omission has been made, please bring this to the publisher's attention so that proper acknowledgement may be given in future editions.

The views expressed in this book are not necessarily those of the publisher.

British Library Cataloguing in Publication Data applied for
ISBN 978-1-912480-88-3

Baking

Real

Bread

Family recipes
with stories and songs
for celebrating bread

Warren Lee Cohen

Hawthorn Press

Contents

Dedication

This book is dedicated to all those inspiring bread bakers, young and old, with whom I have had the privilege of kneading dough, and especially to Luciana who is wonderful leaven for my soul.

Acknowledgements

Special thanks to Julie Gritten for generously contributing the chapter on gluten free recipes and to Rupert Dunn for his appendix on building a real bread culture. I would like to thank Floris Books for their permission to include three poems from *Prayers and Graces*: Before the flour, the mill; Earth who gives to us this food; and Grace over the meal.

I would like to thank Colin Price and Songbird Press for permission to include three compositions from his book, *Let's Sing and Celebrate*.

I would also like to thank the following individuals whose kind help, support and creative contributions have been an immense help in bringing together the diverse content of this book.

Marije Rowling, illustrator and collaborator
Elisabeth Winkler, editor
Martin Large, publisher, whose bold questions
 inspired this book
Beverly McCartney
Christine Fynes-Clinton
Cinnie Blaire
Erica Grantham
Gabrielle Dietrich
Jill Taplin
Julie Ziegler
Karin Jarman
Kate Hammond
Kathy Brunetta
Luciana Baptista
Michael Moran
Simone Horowitz
Susanna Segnit
Thais Bishop
Wendy Causey
Wendy Cook
Lost Valley Educational Center
Olympia Waldorf School
Emerson College kitchen and community

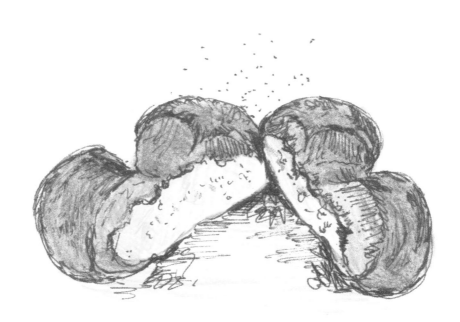

Foreword

To bake is to live –
to share bread is to love

How quickly we have traded baking bread, this most instinctive of human activities, for convenience. This book's value is beyond measure if it helps you to connect with baking and children become part of this.

Take two ingredients, a ground cereal and some water, make a paste and bake over an open fire, and you have food that will sustain you through the lean months. Anything else added into the mix or to enhance the method can, if done with consideration, yield a more civilised loaf.

Our shared ancestry of farming, taming beasts, harnessing water and wind power, encapsulating fire in an oven, and in fact most of our early progress and advancement, during peaceable times, was driven by the need for plentiful and edible bread.

A loaf on the table when we share a meal sings to us of this well-being. To be equipped to provide this loaf yourself while involving children with putting it there, is surely one of life's joys. It will require from you: nurturing, waiting, kneading, watching,

tapping. This effort is hugely rewarded by bread's impact on our senses, something we absorb and carry with us through life.

Baking Real Bread reflects the spirit of bread-making, and the imprint left on cultures across the world. The stories, poems, recipes and pictures will serve us as a well-honed springboard from which to dive arms first (sleeves rolled up) into the making and baking and sharing that will be the legacy of this exquisite book.

As a child growing up in Hobbs House above my family's bakery in the Cotswold High Street of Chipping Sodbury, my earliest memories are a blend of exciting sensations. Sneaking down at 4am during the summer holidays to watch my Dad work amongst billowing clouds of flour, accompanied by the whir of mixing machines, buzzers and the latest Bruce Springsteen cassette, his hands and arms working deftly. This visual manifestation presenting itself to rubbed- awake eyes was layered with the intoxicating smell of the sourdough tub and the invigorating aroma of steaming loaves being tipped out of the oven. Particularly fondly, I recollect the triumph of finally being old enough to jam and sugar the doughnuts, and over-filling the last one as a degustible reward for myself. The connection with those early morning efforts, followed shortly by the queue out the door with customers eager to buy the morning's produce, paved the way for me to pursue the craft.

Bread-making gives and gives. Now a father of four, I count as amongst the memorable times of my life the moments shared with Milo, Beatrix, Josephine and Prudence, immersing ourselves in the making of bread, waffles or pizza. I have found we were all inspired by the stories in this book, and when it is time to make bread we lose ourselves in a world of mixing and kneading.

So take up the book and absorb it from cover to cover, and I implore you to promise a child or two that there will be some baking, and get stuck in. There is very little to lose and a huge amount to be gained. Resist exacting perfection and meticulous attention to detail. Instead celebrate the entire messy and tasty process, connecting with an intuitive desire to create and share.

Well, don't listen to me! Get baking.

Tom Herbert
Co-founder of The Long Table.
Feeding change, one bite at a time.
www.thelongtableonline.com
www.hobbshousebakery.co.uk

Introduction

Welcome to *Baking Real Bread*, an invitation to share the magic of baking bread with children of all ages. Whether you are a beginner or a seasoned hand, this book offers an abundance of information and inspiration to help make baking a satisfying and rich experience. It's a book that you, and the children in your life, will want to share time and again.

Children (adults too!) are deeply impressed by the alchemy of how yeast turns flour, water and salt into bread. This is real life magic. It is an unforgettable experience to bake a beautiful loaf. It touches all our senses and gives feelings of accomplishment, wonder and joy. Baking bread is meaningful work that teaches a diverse set of skills and offers bountiful rewards.

I have gathered recipes from over 30 years of baking bread at home, workshops and schools. Designed for parents, teachers and children, this practical and comprehensive guide has everything you need to get started: all the bread basics for beginners and a variety of recipes to give you confidence to bake at home or school. People on restricted diets are catered for with wheat-free and gluten-free recipes. I also show how to make bread rise without commercial yeast using your own sourdough starter.

But this is more than a recipe book. Baking bread without engaging the imagination is hard work. Add imagination, and the activity becomes fun and deeply nourishing on other levels. I have collected a store of multicultural tales, songs and blessings to bring baking to life. These are so enriching that I have placed the recipes right between the stories, and blessings, making a hearty sandwich.

The bread stories precede the recipes, while the songs, poems and blessings come after. Kneading the imagination enriches a child's baking experience making it both formative and memorable. More about these benefits are in the first chapter, 'What baking bread brings to children'.

After sharing recipes and a lively bread culture of stories, songs and poems, I offer suggestions for bread-related projects and educational activities. This section will be of special interest to teachers, adventurous parents and home schoolers. I start with instructions on how to build an earthen bread oven. A wood-fired oven makes a profound impression on all that create and bake with one.

In the chapter 'Enlivening the senses', I explore how our human senses develop and the role that bread-baking can play in supporting their healthy growth. The following chapter includes suggestions for incorporating bread-baking into the school curriculum. From mathematics to nutrition, creative writing to geography, baking bread can bring a vast array of subjects to life. A list of resources including relevant websites is included in the bibliography.

I then dedicate a chapter to the seven traditional grains that feed most of the world's people. Each grain has a unique story to tell, connected with its origin, mythology, nutritional profile and the people that rely upon it. Each one has helped shape specific cultures, diets, customs and rituals. The grains are central to understanding world civilizations. Included are menu suggestions for how to incorporate all of these grains into a healthy and varied diet.

Home-baked bread creates a healthy alternative to industrially produced, sliced white bread. The chapter 'Factory-made bread – wheat sensitivities, allergies and coeliac disease' has suggestions for finding the diet that best suits you, including recommendations for using grains other than wheat. I also examine some of the health issues surrounding food today and share some nutritional insights.

I have included an appendix by the Soil Association former editor, Elisabeth Winkler, that explains the virtues of using fresh, organic and biodynamic ingredients.

How I started baking

My own interest in baking bread developed years ago for the most unlikely of reasons. I wanted to make life-sized sculptures of animals and people. I settled with a chuckle on the idea of making them out of bread because they would naturally decompose, be inexpensive, and fun to create.

Bread has always intrigued me. It is the staff of life, an everyday food of the people. And at the same time, this staple can be transformed, through certain religious practices, to embody the presence of God. Bread is both a down-to- earth food, and the most sacred of substances. This makes it very special indeed.

My 'BREADMAN' sculptures were surprisingly successful in galleries and museums across the United States. They were a lot of fun as well. I decided that I wanted to provide my baking assistants with tasty and nourishing bread while we worked. And so, I began to learn not just bread art, but also the art of baking bread to eat. This has turned into a passion, and I have been baking bread, building bread ovens and teaching bread workshops ever since. And, wherever I go, I have found that people love fresh bread and are invigorated by the activity of baking it.

Inspired by my artistic and practical working with bread, I wrote creative stories, including the children's picture book *Dragon Baked Bread* (published by Steiner Books, further details at the end of this book). That, in turn, has led to the one you now hold in your hands.

Enduring memories

As a part of my research for this book, I have talked with many parents and teachers about their bread-baking experiences. I have sprinkled their anecdotes throughout the book, adding some spice and perhaps a little wisdom. It has been fascinating to discover that if people baked at all as children, they usually have retained enjoyable and vivid memories. When I asked one 40-year-old man if he had ever baked as a child, his face lit up:

'When I was growing up in Brazil, my family would spend the summer in the countryside. An old woman used to take care of us children and cook for us. When she saw my brother, sister and me, she would invite us to her side as she kneaded the bread dough. I liked watching her skillful hands pressing the dough and then folding it over and over again. When it was time to shape the loaves, she would always pinch off three bits of dough and shape them into little angel loaves. They were special – our very own loaves, kid-sized and just for us.'

Other people's remembrances touch a similarly deep place. People recall the joy of feeling purposeful and the satisfaction of accomplishment. Their experience of baking as a child clearly enriched their upbringing and the memories continue to nourish them to this day.

Steiner/Waldorf education

You will find many references in this book to Steiner/Waldorf education. Although I have taught in state, private and home school settings, I have devoted most of my professional career to working in Steiner/Waldorf schools and training their teachers. Much of my inspiration comes from these experiences. The developmental approach pioneered in Waldorf schools is guided by the teachings of the Austrian philosopher Rudolph Steiner (1861-1925).

Recently I was talking with my 14-year -old daughter about ways that we measure time. We were getting a bit silly, so I asked her, 'How many loaves old are you?' She pondered this a while and then we set out together to do some figuring. I have been baking for my family on average four loaves of bread every week for her entire life: 4 loaves x 52 weeks x 14 years = 2912. 'You are fast approaching 3000 loaves old and that does not even include pizzas, focaccias, cinnamon buns, muffins or crescents!'

Steiner saw that a child's imagination and enthusiasm had to be fully engaged to learn effectively, as I explain in the chapter 'Enlivening the senses'.

Art, music, movement and handicrafts alongside academic studies are integral aspects of educating the whole child. Through this balanced approach not only is academic learning fostered, but the children's physical, emotional, social, intellectual and spiritual needs are cared for as well. It is often said, 'Waldorf education is an education of the head, heart and hands'. The purposeful activity of baking bread helps exercise this dynamic balance of thinking, feeling and doing. A list of useful resources and websites, including my own, are included in the bibliography.

Bakers create not only delicious bread to eat. They also leaven the very substance of their beings. Baking makes the baker. The mind is nourished through delighting in what the senses bring to its attention. And the spirit is fed by images that enrich its understanding of the alchemical transformation of flour, water, salt and yeast into bread. Baking has been a real joy in my life, at home, in the classroom and workshops. I hope that you too will experience the many benefits this ancient activity can bring.

Warren Lee Cohen
Toronto, Canada

Chapter One

What baking bread brings to children

Baking bread with children can be a wonderful and lively experience, even more than a lesson in cooking. It has the potential to weave together many of the important aspects of life, to strengthen their skills and abilities and to harness their abundant energy. The whole culture of bread-baking, its recipes, stories, songs and poems educates children and supports their healthy development.

Where food comes from

In the past, children knew how bread was made because the whole baking process was a regular part of daily life. Throughout Europe there was at least one bakery in every village, and everyone had direct contact with its gentle warmth and smell. The white lined wrinkles on the baker's hands were a familiar sight to customers who bought their freshly baked bread straight from the oven. The work of all the people involved, including the farmer, miller, and shopkeeper, were visible for all to see.

Today, few of us know where our food comes from. Food production has been removed from our sight into larger and more remote factories. From a child's perspective, bread appears neatly stacked on shelves and wrapped in plastic. One man told me that he was 18 before he discovered how bread was actually made. He had eaten it most days of his life without ever inquiring how this squidgy white loaf appeared in its plastic wrapper. This is an all- too-common experience.

Luckily children are by nature curious and yearn to know more about everything they encounter. By showing them the practical crafts that are part of our daily survival, we can give them tools for life. Baking bread is one such skill. You can teach it by baking alongside children. Imitation is a natural way that children come to learn new knowledge and abilities.

Kneading the imagination

Stories fire the imagination. There are few things children love more than listening to stories, singing songs and then acting them out. Some could do this all day. A child's imagination has immense value and is essential to learning. Playing allows children to digest and integrate all that they are experiencing through their senses. They are learning by doing and entering into this process with their entire beings.

I have found that telling a story before engaging children in bread-making (or indeed any activity) allows them to participate even more deeply in it. While children are working the dough with their hands, they are also kneading their imaginations. It is the pictorial images in particular that fill children with wonder, awe and create an image-rich framework, to which they can relate their own experiences. Stories invite a child's whole creative being to become involved. Storytelling and bread baking leaven one another. These experiences become not only enduring memories, but also form the basis for a vast array of cognitive and manual skills.

Songs and stories help children make compassionate connections with other people's lives. They enrich the whole learning process. Listening to stories about the farmer, the miller and the baker teach children how essential each person is in all the essential work needed so that we can have our daily bread. Similarly, a blessing for the sun shining on the wheat and a song about harvest time stimulate a child's understanding of how the world works, and how everything fits together. Ours is a world of interdependence and everyone and everything has something valuable to contribute.

By combining these imaginative activities with baking bread, a child's intellectual grasp is grounded in the physical act of baking. Children are using feelings and thoughts, as well as actions, in a playful and purposeful way. So, hands, hearts and heads are involved, and the balance between all three aids a child's well-rounded development.

The many natural breaks in bread-making lend themselves to interludes of song and storytelling. As you wait for the yeast to activate, dough to rise, bread to cook and then cool, stories, poems, songs and blessings can be kneaded right in. These will stir the bakers' enthusiasm while their hands are busy doing the work. Nothing brings me more joy than a kitchen filled with song and the aromas of fresh bread in the making.

Bread dough can also be modelled and sculpted. Children are easily inspired to make animals, letters, numbers or other forms out of living dough. It is a wonderful way to learn the alphabet. They will also enjoy shaping their loaves inspired by something they have seen in nature, a leaf, snail, or by some imagined creation. Baking bread in this way allows them a practical outlet for connecting their rich inner lives with their developing skills and abilities. It is important work. And besides that, it's fun!

Creating a home

Fresh baked bread fills a home with rich earthy aromas. Its scent makes mouths water as stomachs prepare to digest the sustenance to come.

Common wisdom says if you want to give guests a warm welcome, bake bread before they arrive. The smell of baking gives a house a palpable aura of care, comfort and security. It enlivens people's sense of well-being, to which children are the most sensitive of all. A home with an active and creative kitchen culture is one where a child feels nurtured. Home is where the hearth is, and few foods remind one of this more than fresh baked bread. Thus, hearth and heart, which share a common linguistic root, become one. A whole mood of creative nurturing can be fostered and children naturally want to join in and help with the baking.

As children get older (say from the age of nine) they can readily learn to carry out the entire baking process from start to finish with only a little support from adults. They can begin to read and follow recipes, accurately measure ingredients, set the oven, knead and form the loaves, then wait the required

intervals. When the bread is done, they will serve it with pride, their sense of accomplishment tangible. This is a practical way that children can contribute to the family home, gaining both recognition and independence.

Healthy eating

Baking bread can also encourage healthy eating. Many parents are concerned that their children are not getting all the nutrition they need and struggle finding good food their children will eat. However, I have seen time and again that if children have helped to cook food or to bake their own bread, if they have listened to imaginative stories and waited with anticipation for the food to be ready, then their natural hunger will be piqued.

Cooking with children is an effective way of improving and broadening their diets. Home-baked bread is energy-rich and sustaining with none of the chemicals and additives found in shop-bought bread. It can be made even more nutritious if you choose recipes with whole grains, fruits and nuts. Some children might not like the taste at first, especially if they are not used to it. But once children start baking, they may well open up to new tastes and textures. Once they see you enjoying an unusual food and not making a big deal about it, they are more likely to try some too.

How we are connected –
being involved from start to finish

Children can experience an interconnected world when we encourage them to see (and participate) in a whole process from start to finish. When each step is visibly linked with the one that went before, a real understanding of connection arises. Baking bread helps children to see this. They can begin to grasp how every slice of toast is linked to the work of others – the people who grow the wheat, bake the bread, transport the loaves, sell the bread, manufacture the toaster, provide the electricity for the toaster, and so on. Our world is interconnected through trade, and we are remarkably dependent on people we might never meet, and they are equally dependent on us.

Children can best appreciate the reality of this interdependence if we take time to show them all the work that goes into making a loaf of bread – and then stand back and let them do their bit. As I explain in the chapter 'Bread projects and educational activities', children can be involved right from the start, by sowing some grains and watching how they grow. They can learn how to harvest, thresh and winnow (separating the grain from the chaff), then grind the grains into flour to make bread. If time, energy and physical space allow, building a bread oven is another powerful way of seeing a process through from start to finish (instructions for building your own oven start on page 157).

There is so much valuable and meaningful work that can be done in connection with baking bread. Do whatever aspects you can fit into your schedule. While it can take months to go from sowing grains to grinding them into flour, simply baking with children and reading a story can take as little as an hour.

Establish a rhythm

Many of us lead full and busy lives and it can seem daunting to find time to bake bread with our children. Let me assure you that this will be time well spent. Children love this activity, and you will have plenty of good bread to eat. It is a simple way to do good work, side by side with your child, and to nurture your family on all levels.

Many bread-baking families I know create a rhythm by baking once a week. Some parents I know choose Saturday as their special day, but any day will work, especially if it's the same one each week. A regular rhythm really does make it easier to bake bread, or to do anything for that matter. This gives structure to the week and enough time for preparation. It won't be long before you and the children are carried by the routine you have created. Having a special day also allows a child's anticipation to grow. All week long they will look forward to baking day, knowing that they can help make and eat fresh bread on that special day.

In many Steiner/Waldorf kindergartens the children recognise the days of the week not so much by their names, Monday, Tuesday, Wednesday, but by the activity associated with them. One is painting day, another is music day, and, invariably, a very popular one is baking day. Children like knowing what to expect. This helps them feel more in control of their lives. It gives them a sense of safety and security. So, when it is baking day and they see all the ingredients prepared, they know what will happen next and exactly how they can be helpful.

Imitation

'I give my two-year-old grandchild a seat at the table and then mix and knead my dough right in front of her watchful eyes. When it is ready, I give her a piece to knead along with me. She does it just like Grandma, pressing her hands into the soft warm dough. This is real work for a young child.' A grand-mother on baking with her two-year-old granddaughter.

Young children long to master their world, to do all the things they see adults around them doing. When they see mother cook or father clean, they are naturally impelled to engage in the same activity. They want to discover through doing how to become a full human being, to learn all the skills needed to grow up. In their play, they will endlessly imitate everything they see around them, regardless, as we may at times dismay, of its worthiness of being copied. They will do it anyway, because this

is how they can gain the skills they need. Our task as adults is to surround young children with activity worthy of imitation. This is formative education and children will soak it right up.

This phase of imitation is a natural mode of learning for young children up to the age of seven, after which it gradually diminishes. Take advantage of this window of opportunity by introducing them to traditional crafts: the practical work that allows them to engage meaningfully in making a house (or school) a home. These can include cooking, cleaning, sewing and making simple, useful items. In this way, children learn both the craft itself, and how to make a valuable contribution. They grow in confidence because they are gaining an adult skill, and one that develops a child's potential (see the chapter 'Enlivening the senses'). No activity is more suitable and confidence-building than baking bread.

So, bake bread with your children. Try not to rush, but do things in a rhythmical and relaxed way. Children naturally want to participate when an adult is having fun. Add a song or a story, and they will clamour to join in. Ultimately, the enjoyment of baking is as important as the loaf produced. You can taste that joy in the final product. As the poet Kahlil Gibran said, 'Work is love made visible'. What better gift can you offer a child?

Lunch at the nature café

One morning break, I got an intriguing invitation from the children in the school where I teach. A young girl ran out of breath to fetch me. 'Mr Cohen! Mr Cohen! Will you please come for lunch at our nature café?'

Places were set on various tree stumps. Courteous young waiters came by to take my order. They relayed them to the kitchen where the orders were prepared by a team of cooks. There was a lot of giggling in the kitchen, as the nature chefs perfected their creations. At last my food was served. It was beautifully arranged on a leaf plate and decorated with wild flowers. I pretended to eat it while I talked with other guests. Then, as if unable to eat another bite of such delicious food, I paid for my meal with five acorns.

The children (more than a dozen eight, nine and ten-year-olds) had been playing this game for days, building a kitchen from sticks and leaves and then making pretend food from leaves, mud and wild flowers. They had concocted the most artistic creations: soup, bread and salad and for dessert, baked fruit pies, all made with their imaginations, and hard work.

It was so satisfying to enter into their play world. Through their creativity, they had transformed what they were learning into life-serving knowledge.

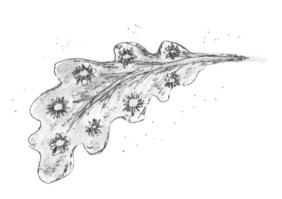

Chapter Two

Bread stories

These bread stories come from storytellers whose traditions span the globe, passed down by word of mouth from generation to generation. I have so enjoyed collecting these that I have been inspired to write a few of my own.

Read them aloud or, better yet, use your own words. Telling stories is an excellent preparation for baking with children. Stories awaken their curiosity, imagination and eagerness to bake. They can also be shared during the natural pauses in the baking process. Allow the creative images from these stories

to live as leaven, to bring levity and meaning to your baking experience. They will lighten the whole process – and even the final loaves!

The first seven stories are particularly suited to younger children up to seven years of age. Their themes and images are universal. They have the quality of fairy tales or simple nature stories, which young children simply drink in. The remaining stories have a more awake or intellectual quality and involve trickery. They will appeal more to questions that directly live in older children.

A grain of wheat
A story by the author about how seeds grow

Deep within the dark cold earth, a seed was peacefully sleeping. Blanketed by the soft soil and a fine layer of snow, the seed slept on and on. Not even an earthworm carelessly bumping into it could awaken it from its deep slumber. Until one day it felt a little tickle on its seed coat, a warm little tickle. It began to wake up and ever so slightly it stretched and swelled and stretched and swelled and eventually began to slip out of its old seed coat. Then it could hear the call of spring, the most beautiful music coming from far, far away. Perhaps it was the pitter-patter of warm rain falling upon the earth or the dancing movements of the stars in the heavens, which humans no longer hear, but plants still can. It delighted to hear it and swelled with eagerness to grow into a plant.

Now the seed was truly awake. Slipping out of its seed coat, it pushed its roots deep into the earth. When it had a firm footing, the seed forced itself through the soil, right up into the daylight where it opened its first tender green leaf. It was a small start, but soon it sent out another leaf and another. Day after day, leaf after leaf, it grew straight up towards the sun. With each day it grew bigger and stronger. It stretched ever higher to reach the sun's golden glow.

But try as it may, the plant could not reach all the way, so it decided to make the sun a special gift instead. For many days the plant stored up all of its energy, until it felt it could hold no more. And then it packed all of its energy into tiny little balls. These swelled day by day and soon became large and hard. They were the richest treasures that the plant could make, its very own seeds, and it offered them to the sun. The sun was so grateful to receive these that it shone even more brightly and helped to turn them golden brown. The plant was well pleased and lay down to rest.

And when at last summer passed into autumn, the plant gave these seeds to the earth for safe keeping until the next spring. And so the seed's seeds lay sleeping, deep within the dark cold earth, until the next call of spring should awaken them from their slumber.

Why grains are so small
A legend from India

Back in the days when the earth was still young, things were more harmonious than they are now. Men and women were stronger and more beautiful. Animals lived together in peace, and fruit from the trees was plentiful and sweet. People ate rice as their main food. The rice grains were so large that just one grain of rice was enough to feed an entire family.

The earth was bountiful in those days and it was little work for the people to gather all the food they needed. When the rice was heavy and ripe, it fell off on its own from the stalks. It rolled into the villages and even rolled up into the granaries. Filled with gratitude, the people sang about the generosity of nature.

One year when the rice was larger and more plentiful than ever before, an old widow said to her daughter, 'Our granaries are too small. We shall build larger ones.'

They pulled the old granaries down and lay stone atop stone to build new granaries. Just at that time, the rice was ripe in the fields and ready to fall off. Great haste was made, but the rice came rolling in while the work was still going on. Frustrated, the widow struck a grain with her hand and cried, 'Could you not wait in the fields until the granaries are ready? Do not bother us yet! We are not ready.'

In an instant the rice shattered into a thousand pieces and said, 'From this day forth, we rice grains will wait in the fields until we are wanted. You will have to gather us by yourselves.'

Since that time all grains have become smaller, smaller even than fruits, and the people of the earth must gather them into their granaries by their own hard efforts. So it is today.

Little red hen
Folktale from Russia

Once upon a time there was a little red hen who lived in a barn full of hay. She lived with her friends, a rat, a cat and a pig. One day Little Red Hen went for a walk in the fields and found some grains of wheat. She took them back to the barn and asked her friends if they would help her plant the grains of wheat in the earth.

'Who will help me plant the wheat?' asked Little Red Hen.
'Not I,' said the rat.
'Not I,' said the cat.
'Not I,' said the pig.
'Then I will plant the grains of wheat by myself,' said Little Red Hen.

And so she did. She trotted off to the well-ploughed field and planted the grains of wheat.

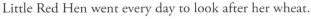

Little Red Hen went every day to look after her wheat.
She saw it grow stronger and taller by the day. By the end of the summer it was golden and swaying in the breeze. It was ready for harvesting, so she went off to ask her friends if they would help her to cut the wheat.

'Who will help me to harvest the wheat?' asked Little Red Hen.
'Not I,' said the rat.
'Not I,' said the cat.
'Not I,' said the pig.
'Then I will cut the wheat by myself,' said Little Red Hen.

And so she did. She swung her sickle and cut each stalk by herself. She tied them together into little bundles. Little Red Hen wanted to take the golden grain to the old wooden windmill and ask the miller to grind the wheat into flour. She asked her friends if they would help her carry the wheat.

'Who will help me take the wheat to the miller?' asked Little Red Hen.
'Not I,' said the rat.
'Not I,' said the cat.
'Not I,' said the pig.
'Then I will take the wheat by myself,' she said.

And so she did. She carried all of the wheat to the windmill all by herself. The miller poured the wheat into his mill and ground it all into flour. Then he put it in a sack for Little Red Hen to carry. She went back to the farmyard and asked her friends if they would help her to take the flour to the baker.

'Who will help me to take the flour to the baker to be baked into bread?' asked Little Red Hen.
'Not I,' said the rat.
'Not I,' said the cat.
'Not I,' said the pig
'Then I will take the flour to the baker myself,' said Little Red Hen.

And so she did. Little Red Hen dragged the sack of flour all the way to the baker's shop. The baker made the flour into bread dough and popped it in the oven. While it was baking they had a nice chat over a cup of tea. When the bread was ready the baker put the loaves in a special net bag for Little Red Hen to carry home. When Little Red Hen reached the farmyard she asked her friends who would help her to eat the bread.

'Who will help me eat the bread?' asked Little Red Hen.
'Mmm! I will,' said the rat.
'Mmm! I will,' said the cat.
'Mmm! I will,' said the pig.
'Oh no you won't!' said Little Red Hen.

'All by myself I planted the wheat, watched it grow and cut it down. All by myself I took the grain to the miller to be ground into flour. All by myself I took the flour to the baker to be baked into bread. And now all by myself I will eat the bread.'

And so she did.

The hedgehog and his bride
Folktale from Lithuania

Once upon a time there was an old broom maker, whose beard was as coarse as the bristles he used for his brooms. One day he went to the forest to gather switches, when all of a sudden a hedgehog appeared on his path. Back and forth the hedgehog scurried, running round and around the old broom maker. It stayed with him the whole day. When the old man sat down to eat, the hedgehog bustled about at his feet grateful for any breadcrumbs that fell. The old broom maker took a liking to the prickly little animal. He picked him up, put him in his cap and brought him home.

In the morning when the old man and his wife woke up, they were surprised by how clean and neat their little house had become. All the plates had been washed and placed carefully in the cupboards. The pots and pans had been scrubbed till they shone. The floor had been swept clean. Fresh water had been brought in, and the firewood had been chopped and stacked neatly by the stove. And there was the hedgehog sitting on a stool, busily at work sewing the old man's trousers using a needle from his own back.

The old man and his wife were so pleased with the hedgehog that they decided to keep him as a son, whom they named Prickly. Prickly grew up as part of their family, and when he was old enough they thought of finding him a wife. But, it was not just any maiden that Prickly wanted to marry. He only wanted the king's daughter! He begged his new father to go to the king and ask for the king's daughter's hand in marriage on his behalf. The father loved Prickly dearly, and so went to the king.

The king received the old broom maker and heard his request. He too loved his daughter and so asked the old broom maker to bring his son to the palace so that he could weigh up the young man's virtues.

The old man came home and told Prickly all about it. They both put on their finest clothes and returned to meet the king. The king took one look at Prickly, the proposed bridegroom, and burst out laughing until his belly nearly burst. 'This is the bridegroom for my daughter!' cried the king between fits of laughter.

Not knowing what else to do, the old man began praising the hedgehog, saying how clever and hardworking he was. 'We'll see,' said the king. Then after a pause, he continued, 'I'll consider this marriage on one condition. Your son, Prickly, must plough my fields, grind the grain and then bake golden loaves out of the flour, enough to feed the whole palace.'

The old broom maker listened and was filled with sorrow. How would the hedgehog be able to do all this work all by himself, he wondered? But Prickly was ready to begin at once. Without hesitation the hedgehog asked his father to take him to the king's land. He immediately began scurrying up and down the unploughed field. As he did so he cried out, 'Field, field, come to life and plough yourself!' At that very moment the field was ploughed. Then he cried, 'Field, field, come to life and harrow yourself!'

And at once the field was harrowed, its soil broken up fine and smooth. Then he cried, 'Field, field, come to life and stretch into furrows!' And at once, the furrows stretched across the field straight as strings. And at his next call, grains of wheat dropped from the sky into the neat furrows and were gently blanketed with soil.

Prickly took a short rest and then cried, 'Wheat, wheat, come to life, grow and ripen, golden wheat!' At once the wheat grew from the soil. As it rose above the ground, it turned from green to gold and it was ripe. 'Wheat, wheat, come to life and gather into golden sheaves!' cried Prickly.

The wheat cut and gathered itself into tall sheaves that dried instantly in the sun. Prickly then called out, 'Wheat, wheat, come to life, thresh yourself and then grind yourself into fine flour!'

Soon the grain was threshed and ground into fine flour. And finally the hedgehog cried, 'Wheat, wheat, come to life and bake yourself into golden loaves!' And so the wheat mixed with water and yeast hopped into the red-hot ovens and came out as beautiful golden loaves. At Prickly's next command the loaves climbed into wagons and rode off to the king's palace ready to feed all of his subjects. A hundred wagonloads they made in all, and the hedgehog, curled up in a ball, rolled ahead of them pointing out the way.

When the king saw all that the hedgehog had done, he summoned his daughter, showed her the bridegroom and told her to get ready for the wedding. The princess did not like the sight of the hedgehog, but could not disobey her father's wishes. She married Prickly and was soon in for quite another surprise.

Late on the night after their wedding feast when his young bride had gone to sleep, Prickly cast off his prickly skin. He carefully hid it behind the stove. Underneath he was a handsome young man; so handsome in fact that he seemed to give a glow to everything around him, like the sun. After a fitful night's sleep, the king's daughter opened her eyes and was overjoyed to see the handsome young man in place of the hedgehog. She cried with joy. At daybreak Prickly climbed back into his hedgehog skin and behaved as usual. But as soon as it was night-time, he cast off his sharp needles and turned back into a handsome young man. Together they kept this secret and lived happily ever after.

Grandmother Maize
A Cherokee legend

Long ago when the world was still young, an old woman, Grandmother, lived together with her grandson.

Their home was in the forest at the foot of the big mountain next to a bubbling spring. Nature was generous. They had plenty to eat and lived together happily.

When the boy reached his seventh year, Grandmother gave him his first bow and arrow. He went into the forest to hunt and that evening carried back a small bird that he had caught.

Grandmother was proud of Grandson and told him, 'You will be a great hunter. Today you have provided for both of us. Someday you will feed a whole nation! We shall have a feast.' She went into her small storehouse behind the cabin and came out with a basket full of dried maize. She cooked this together with the bird and made a delicious supper. They ate and then they went to sleep contented.

From that day on Grandson went out to hunt and each night he presented his catch to Grandmother. She went into her storehouse, brought out a basketful of dried maize and made supper for the two of them. And the food was always delicious.

One day the boy was curious to see where Grandmother kept the maize and he peeked into the storehouse. To his surprise, the storehouse was empty, completely empty. There was nothing in there and certainly no store of maize. Yet that same evening, when he returned from the forest, she went in to the storehouse and brought out a basket filled with dried maize for their supper. Grandson became very curious indeed and decided that he must discover how Grandmother brought maize from an empty storehouse.

On the following day, he carried home his catch as usual. When Grandmother went into the storehouse to bring the maize, he sneaked up to the side of the house and peaked between the cracks in the walls. There he saw another surprising sight. Inside the empty house, he saw Grandmother place the basket on the floor between her feet. He watched as she then rubbed her belly up and down with both hands. Dried maize fell from her body and filled the basket to the top.

The boy grew scared at what he had seen. Was she a spirit, he wondered? He quickly retreated back from the storehouse and pretended to be waiting for supper. But Grandmother could see by the look on his face that he had witnessed her secret. She asked him, 'Grandson, have you seen how I fill the basket with maize each evening?'

'Yes, Grandmother,' the honest boy replied.

With a tear in her eye, the old woman replied, 'Well then I must prepare to leave you. For now that you know my secret, I can no longer live on this earth. By sunrise tomorrow, I will be dead. But, if you listen carefully and do as I say, you will be able to feed yourself, and many others as well.'

The boy was scared and came to hug his grandmother, but she motioned him away. 'It is too late. We cannot change what has come to pass. Do exactly as I say. Clear a patch of land on the sunny side of the house. Make sure that the brown earth is flat and free of all plants. Then take my dead body and drag it across the patch seven times. Make seven furrows and then bury my body at the head of the patch. Watch the earth carefully and keep the earth clear. If you follow my directions then you will see me again and be able to feed the people.' Grandmother stopped speaking. She lay down to rest and by sunrise had left her body.

Grandson did exactly as she had told him. He cleared the plants from a large patch of land next to the house and smoothed out the moist brown earth until it was perfectly flat and bare. He dragged her body across the patch seven times, making seven furrows and then buried her body at the head of the patch. Wherever a drop of her blood had touched the earth, a small plant sprouted up. These delicate green shoots soon grew and grew into strong plants. The boy made sure to keep the earth bare between the plants. They soon grew taller than he was. And as they stretched towards the sun, he could faintly hear his grandmother's voice whispering in their leaves. Grandson was comforted by her familiar voice as she reminded him how to care for the plants with water from the spring.

As the days grew shorter and colder, ears of maize formed on each plant. Brown silk like Grandmother's own hair shone from each ear. He had worked hard and now Grandmother's promise had come true. The maize was sweet and filling. He was happy once more. For he now knew that Grandmother had become the maize plant. And that maize would keep the Cherokee people strong forever.

Gingerbread Man
Folktale from Europe

Once upon a time there lived an old man and an old woman who had no children. So they decided to bake a gingerbread man. They shaped him ever so carefully with big bright eyes, strong limbs and a full mouth. When they took him out of the oven, they were happy. But no sooner had he cooled down, than he jumped off the counter and began to run away.

'Come back!' called the old man. 'Please do stay,' cried the old woman.

But the gingerbread man just laughed and said, 'Run, run as fast as you can! You can't catch me! I'm the gingerbread man!'

And they chased him around and around the kitchen and out into the yard, but they could not catch him.

The gingerbread man ran and ran and ran. He ran past a cow grazing in the meadow.

The cow said, 'Mmm! A gingerbread man. Are gingerbread men sweeter than grass? Could I have a nibble from your arm?'

The gingerbread man just laughed and said, 'Run, run as fast as you can! You can't catch me! I'm the gingerbread man!' And the cow could not catch him.

The gingerbread man ran and ran and ran. He ran past a ram in a pasture.

The ram said, 'Mmm! A gingerbread man. I have heard that gingerbread men are delicious. Could I have a bite from your leg?'

But the gingerbread man just laughed and said, 'Run, run as fast as you can! You can't catch me! I'm the gingerbread man!' And the ram could not catch him.

The gingerbread man ran and ran and ran, until he came to a river. Just then a fox walked by and said, 'Mmm! A gingerbread man. They are tasty. Could I have a bit of your hat?'

But the gingerbread man just laughed and said, 'Run, run as fast as you can! You can't catch me! I'm the gingerbread man!'

'Maybe I can't catch you,' said the fox, taking a step closer. 'But if you try to cross the river, you will surely get wet and crumble to pieces.
Come, hop on my tail, and I will carry you across.' So, the gingerbread man did just that.

As the fox began to swim across the river, his tail dipped into the water. 'Oh dear! My tail is getting wet. Climb up onto my back to stay dry,' said the fox.

So the gingerbread man did just that. The fox swam on.
But soon he said, 'Oh dear! Now my back is getting wet.
Climb higher onto my nose to stay dry.' So the gingerbread man did just that.

The gingerbread man turned around and looked back.
There he saw the old man, the old woman, the cow,
and the ram, standing on the bank of the river.
He laughed and said, 'Run, run as fast as you can!
You can't catch me! I'm the...'

Then, before the gingerbread man could say another word,
the fox flipped him up into the air and into his open
mouth. And that was the end of the gingerbread man.

Rushen Coatie
Folktale from England

Once upon a time there was a king and a little princess. Her mother, the queen, had been ill and died when the girl was still quite young. Before she died, the queen had told the princess that after she was gone a little red calf would come to her side whenever she wished for anything. All that the little princess needed to do was to ask for the calf's help and her wish would be granted.

After some years the king married again. His new queen was wealthy but ill-natured and had three dreadful daughters, each more mean than the next. Right from the start they hated the little princess who was the apple of the king's eye. They did cruel things to her. They took away all of her fine clothes and made her live by the ash-covered stove in the kitchen. They gave her a dirty old coat made out of rushes and from that day on called her Rushen Coatie.

At suppertime, the mean stepmother kept the poor princess in the kitchen, where she was given only a thimbleful of soup, a grain of barley, a crumb of bread and a thread of meat. When she had eaten all of this, she was still hungry and wished she had more. And so she remembered the little red calf. No sooner had she spoken her wish than the little red calf appeared and told her to put her finger into its left ear. This she did and found some fresh bread. Then the calf told her to put her finger into its right ear, and there she found some nice cheese. These made a filling meal. And so the red calf made sure that the princess had plenty to eat.

The king's wife hoped that Rushen Coatie would soon die from the scant food she received, but she was shocked to see how alive and healthy she was. Rushen Coatie looked better than ever. This made the stepmother meaner and nastier than ever. So she sent one of her daughters to spy upon Rushen Coatie at mealtime. The daughter soon came back, telling of the little red calf **that helped the little princess.**

So the stepmother went to the king and told him that she would like nothing better than to have the meat of a red calf for their supper. The king sent for his butcher who killed and prepared the little red calf. When Rushen Coatie heard the news she sat in the ashes and cried and cried and cried.

Suddenly the dead calf spoke to her and told her to collect all of his bones and to bury them by the side of the kitchen so he could still help her with her wishes. Much cheered, Rushen Coatie gathered all the bones but the shank bone, which she could not find anywhere she looked, and buried them outside the kitchen.

The next day marked the beginning of the Yuletide celebrations. The entire village was preparing their homes and dressing in their finest clothes to go to church. Rushen Coatie also wished that she could go, but her three mean sisters said, 'Why would you want to go to church, you nasty thing? You have to stay at home and tend the fire for supper.'

The cruel stepmother added, 'And you must make us a delicious soup out of a thimbleful of water, a grain of barley and a crumb of bread.'

Rushen Coatie slumped down into the ashes and wept. No sooner had she wished that she could go to church and be free of her cruel stepmother and sisters than she saw the little red calf limping towards her. The poor creature was still missing his shank bone. He told her what to say to the stove so that it would prepare a fine meal. Then he gave her a dress and a pair of crystal slippers to wear and bade her to run off to church. 'All shall be well,' said the little red calf. 'But remember to be the first person back home.'

Off she ran to church. There happened to be a young prince there. When he first caught sight of the little princess in her lovely new dress, he fell in love. After the service, he looked everywhere for her, but she had rushed away to be the first one home. She took off the dress, put on her coat of rushes and stirred the soup the little red calf had made.

When the three sisters arrived back home, they could do nothing but talk about the handsome prince. With much sneering, they shrieked about the beautiful young maiden with whom he had been smitten. They were clearly jealous of her but had no idea that she was in truth, Rushen Coatie. They ignored her and Rushen Coatie was not even welcome at the meal the little red calf had prepared so well. But at least she had a warm feeling in her heart.

The next day the sisters again went to church and again Rushen Coatie was given a thimbleful of water, a grain of barley and a crumb of bread with which to make soup. Again the little red

calf came to her aid and this time gave her an even more beautiful dress to wear with the crystal slippers. When she slipped into the church everyone including the prince admired her beauty. He fell even more in love with her and wanted to find out who she was. But just as the service ended she slipped away, ran back to her home and put back on her coat of rushes. She served the meal that the calf had prepared. All the while she could hear the cruel sisters complaining about the beautiful young woman and the prince who was obviously in love. They were jealous because they too wanted to marry the prince.

Well, the next day the little red calf dressed Rushen Coatie in even finer clothes. She went to church and the handsome prince was there again. He placed a guard by the door so that she could not slip away this time. But, just as the service was over, she took a hop and a run and leapt over the head of the guard and ran all the way home. But as she did so, one of her crystal slippers fell off. She had no time to stop and pick it up, as she had to be the first person home. She quickly laid out the meal and then stood in the ashes by the stove in her coat of rushes. The three ugly sisters talked endlessly about the handsome young prince, who had found the slipper of this mysterious maiden.

The prince sent out a proclamation that whoever could fit the crystal slipper would be his bride. All of the maidens of the court came at once and tried to slip their foot into this little crystal slipper, but it was much too small for all of them. So, he mounted a search throughout the land. From house to house he travelled trying the slipper on the feet of all the young maidens, but none could slide her foot into the little slipper. At last he came to the house of the three ugly sisters. The first tried, but her foot was much too big and lumpy. The second tried too, but could not squeeze her oversized foot into the delicate slipper. In a foul temper the queen hacked off the toes and heel of the third sister so that her foot would fit in the slipper, and it did.

So the prince carried the third sister off to be married; on the back of his white horse. But by the time they had reached the church, the horse's flank had been turned red by the blood that was leaking from the crystal slipper. Filled with disgust, he took her back to her home. There must be someone else who had not tried the slipper.

When they reached the home there stood Rushen Coatie next to the little red calf that had dressed her in the finest dress of all. The prince came towards her and tried the slipper on her little feet. It fitted perfectly. There were gasps of horror and moans from the three nasty sisters and the cruel queen. But the prince had found his bride. He took her by the arm and married her that day. And they lived happily ever after.

The three farmers
Folktale from Europe

Once upon a time in a land neither near nor far lay three fields of grain right next to each other. Wheat grew in all the fields, yet each looked as different as the three farmers that had planted them. The first field was filled with weeds that almost suffocated the wheat. The second field had not a single weed or flower to be seen amongst the perfectly straight rows of wheat. In the third field there were some red poppies and yellow buttercups that looked so beautiful growing amongst the abundant wheat.

When it came time to harvest the fields, just before the feast of St. John on 24th June, the farmers came out early with their wagons, their scythes and their hay forks. The first farmer worked so quickly and carelessly that he did not notice that he was cutting more weeds than wheat, or that he had left many of the sheaves lying in the field. Much of his harvest fell off the wagon as he drove home and what was left he hastily threw into his damp and dirty barn. He was just glad to be done with that job.

The farmer of the second field, which did not have a single weed, was a greedy man. He mowed his field, row by row, as carefully as possible so as not to lose a single grain. He gathered together every sheaf of wheat from his field. Then, as if by mistake, he carefully cut a row from each of his neighbours' fields as well. He loaded all of this onto his wagon and watched the whole way home that none of his harvest should fall off. At home he weighed his harvest and then locked it up in his barn. He then hid the key where only he could find it.

When the third farmer arrived at his field and saw that some of his wheat had been cut, he was not worried. There would still be plenty to feed his family. He sang as he mowed the field and his children played with the poppies and the buttercups. Together they gathered the harvest and headed for home. They carefully loaded the grain into the barn and bade it good night as they closed the barn doors.

A few days later it happened that a poor beggar boy came to the village. He looked tired and hungry as if he had come from afar. He went to each house and asked for a bit of bread. When he knocked at the door of the careless farmer, the farmer had no bread to offer him. So the careless farmer went into his barn to find some wheat, but the new wheat had already begun to rot and could not be used. Sadly the beggar boy walked on and knocked at the door of the greedy farmer.

There he was greeted with a shout, 'I care not for beggars! Go away from my house!'

He dared not tell the hungry boy that his wife was at that very moment baking fresh loaves of bread in the oven. Sadly the beggar boy walked on and knocked at the door of the third farmer.

The third farmer was just thinking about all the sun and rain that it took for his wheat to grow so well, how the health of the plants depended on all the gifts of creation. When he saw the hungry beggar at his door, he said, 'Nature has shared generously with us. We cannot let anyone go hungry.'

He welcomed the boy in and bade him to sit at the table. The third farmer took some new wheat and ground it into flour so that his wife could bake him a good cake. And when it was cooked just right the third farmer, his wife and children sat with the beggar boy and ate with him so that he should not be lonely. All that was left over, they wrapped up for him to take on his journey.

The feast of St. John came and the three farmers walked together to the village. Each carried in his hand a small sack of wheat to give to the fire in thanks for the harvest. An evening mist settled over the valley, a mist so thick that soon the farmers could not see each other.

Soon they could not see their hands or the tips of their own noses. The path grew steeper and steeper. Higher and higher they walked until, tired and exhausted, they came out on top of the white mist. And there they stood in front of three great doors, one very great one in the middle and two smaller ones on either side. Standing in front of the great middle door was a handsome man who looked like the sun itself.

He looked at them with the kindest eyes and asked what they wished to bring him. The greedy farmer hid his little sack behind his back and said, 'Nothing for you! We are three poor farmers coming to thank St. John.'

The handsome man smiled kindly and said, 'Come forward. I am St. John.'

At that the careless farmer pushed forward and presented his sack of half rotten grain. St. John opened it. He saw how dirty and rotten it was, 'This is not your best. It is not a true gift.'

Just then one of the smaller doors opened. Behind it there was a hissing snake. St. John fed the rotten corn to the snake and the door closed.

The greedy farmer stepped forward to offer his little sack. But when the handsome man opened the little sack all he saw were black grains.
He said, 'Stolen grains bring sadness. They will not grow. This is not a true gift.'

Just then the other small door opened. Behind it was a fearsome dragon. He fed these black grains to the dragon and the door closed.

Now it was the third farmer's turn. He barely dared to step forward and offer his gift. But when St. John opened his sack he saw a bright light.

The grains had turned to gold. St. John smiled and asked, 'Have you shared your bread with someone else?'

'Yes,' said the third farmer. 'My wife baked a cake for our family and a poor beggar boy who came to our home.'

The face of St. John grew even more radiant. 'You have given a true gift.'

Just then the great middle door opened and a light as bright as the morning sun shone forth. There stood the same little beggar boy only this time wrapped in golden robes and shining as brightly as the sun and stars together. There he stood by his mother's side. And he spoke, 'I thank you for welcoming me into your home, for giving me bread when I was hungry and for giving me company when I was alone. Your wheat and your home shall be blessed.'

He gave the farmer a handful of wheat and said, 'With an open heart you shall never go hungry.'

The farmer returned to his home and ground the handful of wheat. His wife baked it into good bread. And as long as he lived, this bread fed his family and all the hungry people that came to their home.

The miller's tale
Folktale from Italy

Long ago there was a poor widow with two young children. Her husband had died a few years before and had left them all alone in the world with little to eat. Often they went hungry and they did not know where they would find their next meal. In fact people all across the land were starving, as the harvest that year had been so poor. The widow was desperate to find food for her children and knew that her neighbours had little to give. She led her two children from house to house asking for crusts of bread, but little did they receive in their cold and trembling hands.

Just as all hope was fading, she heard a voice coming from the trunk of a great oak tree. She could not see the source of this voice, but what it said was clear and mysterious. It said, 'Take your children and go to the mill. There you will find plenty of food, warmth and shelter.'

This was strange. She saw no one speaking, and besides, everyone knew that the miller was the stingiest man around. He'd never helped anyone in the village before. But alas, the woman was too tired and too hungry to doubt, so she walked to the mill. A cold rain began to fall making all of them even more miserable, and the youngest began to cry. When at last they arrived at the mill by the banks of the river, they were soaked through. The woman knocked and they waited shivering in the cold a long while.

'What do you want?' bellowed the none-too-welcoming miller. 'Please sir, we are nearly to death with cold and hunger. A bit of bread and shelter until the rain lets up would be a blessing from God.'

'Bah!' cried the miller in a sour mood. 'I have nothing for you and I don't provide gifts from God. If you have no money, I have nothing for you.'

Desperate the woman begged, 'Can't you see that the children are freezing and nearly starved to death? I would pay if I could, but I am a poor widow. Please sir, have mercy on us!'

'Go away from here at once or I'll set my dogs on the lot of you!' he shouted.

Just as the miller's rage was about to burst, an old man appeared from out of nowhere. He doffed his hat, bowed to the poor widow and then tapped the stingy miller with the end of his staff. All at once the miller began to change in the most bizarre and unusual ways. His face grew long. His ears stretched up tall and his teeth stuck out. He sprouted a long brown tail. He dropped onto all fours and let out a loud, 'Hee- haw! Hee-haw!' The miller had turned into a donkey.

Recovering from her shock, the widow realised that the old man was in fact St. Nicholas. He beckoned all of them inside the mill where they found a tasty, hot meal and warm beds waiting for them. 'Now,' he said. 'You will be in charge of the mill.'

The woman protested, as she had no knowledge of how to run a mill. St. Nicholas assured her that everything would be fine, as he would send a helper in the morning. 'All that you need do is to take good care of the customers and charge a price that is fair. You may rent out the donkey for hire. I will return in a year and a day to make sure that all is well.' He bade them good evening, led the dismayed miller-turned-donkey out to the barn, and disappeared into the night.

The woman and children were well surprised by the suddenness of their good fortune. They danced around the table, celebrating the gifts before them: pasta, wedges of creamy cheese, fresh baked bread and garden greens. They had been nearly starving. They said a quick blessing of thanks for their good fortune and sat down to the feast. Never had they tasted food so delicious and satisfying. Soon they were full and tired. They found three beds all made up with soft covers and snuggled in for the best night of sleep they had ever had.

In the morning a young man greeted them. He had been sent by St. Nicholas to help them. He was strong, efficient and knew how to operate the mill. The widow trusted him at once, but still could not understand what she should do about the miller who had been turned into a donkey and now stood in the barn.

And so their new life as millers began. They all worked together. The young man operated the mill. The children tended the donkey and played by the river. And the woman took care of the customers and charged a fair price for grinding their grain. Soon their mill was thriving with more and more customers. And in the evenings, the table was set and the little household shared a hearty meal together. Never had life been so good.

Exactly one year and a day passed. There was a knock at the door and there stood St. Nicholas as promised.

'Now it is time for us to see how the miller is fairing. Let us go to the barn,' he said.

In the barn they saw the poor beast chewing straw. He let out a loud 'Hee-haw!' St. Nicholas tapped him gently with his staff and the donkey slowly began to turn back into the old miller. His long tail disappeared and he stood up rather stiffly on his two legs. His nose and teeth reappeared. Only his ears remained a bit on the long and furry side. They all looked at one another in surprise. St. Nicholas eyed the miller sternly. 'Well now, Miller. Will you take on this woman as your assistant, treat her and her children honourably or would you rather remain a donkey?'

Stumbling over his words the miller said he would take them on as equal partners. 'I see now that I was wrong and stingy. I will take care of them better than my own family and never again will I turn poor people away from my door.'

'Wonderful!' replied St. Nicholas. 'But remember, I do not live far from here and can come back any time if necessary.'

But it never was necessary because the miller had learned his lesson. He treated the woman and her children better than his own family. As he grew older, the miller even gave the mill to them. He became known far and wide as the generous miller, the kindest man around.

The farmer and his sons
A fable from Aesop

A farmer lay ill on his bed. He knew that he would soon die and he wanted to make sure that his three sons would give the same care and attention to his farm as he himself had given to it over the years. He called them to his bedside and whispered urgently, 'My sons, there is a great treasure buried in these fields.'

Soon after his death, the three sons took their shovels and hoes and carefully dug over every portion of their land. They found no treasure. So, they carefully dug every field another time.

Still not finding the buried treasure they dug the fields a third time. Again finding nothing in the fields except soil, they wondered why their elderly father would have tricked them so.

It was not until harvest time that they realised where the treasure lay. For in turning the fields three times, they had brought great fertility to the soil. The harvest of wheat was plentiful and more abundant than ever.

33

Persephone and Demeter
A tale from ancient Greece

Demeter, the goddess of the harvest, had a daughter named Persephone, whose gay laughter was the delight of all the gods. Whenever Demeter went down to earth to tend the trees and fields, Persephone came dancing along. Flowers sprang up from the earth wherever Persephone's feet lightly touched down. Her mother loved her dearly and kept a very close watch on her.

Hades, the god of the underworld, rarely noticed much that happened on earth. But he could not help but fall in love with Persephone, whose beauty pierced even to the dark depths of his world. He wanted this delightful young goddess for his queen. One day, while Persephone was collecting flowers in a meadow far away from her mother, Hades saw his opportunity. The earth trembled and cracked. Hades raced up to the surface of the earth in his dark chariot drawn by four black horses and grabbed Persephone. She was terrified. But before she could scream, they were already racing back through a cleft into the cold, dreary depths of the underworld.

Down and down they went until at last they reached the realm of the dead. There, in that joyless realm, Hades made Persephone his queen. He gave her gold, fine jewels and a throne made from black marble, but none of this brought her any joy. She longed to return to her mother, the sunshine and the world where colourful flowers bloomed.

All was grey in the land of Hades. There was no sun, moon or stars. There were no flowers and no birds to sing of the delights of nature. There was in fact only one tree that bore fruit, a pomegranate. But, Persephone knew she dared not eat any food from the realm of the dead. For she had heard that if she did so, then she would never be allowed to leave. Gradually all hope left her in this dismal grey place, and her heart turned to ice.

Meanwhile, above on the earth, Demeter looked everywhere for her lost daughter. She searched high and low, but could not find her anywhere. Wracked with grief, she could no longer tend the fields and forests of the earth. All of nature wept with her. The flowers wilted, stalks of grain bent to the ground and trees lost all of their leaves.
Nothing would grow while she grieved. Soon the animals and the people were starving for lack of food. The gods begged Demeter to bless the earth once more, but she was too sad. Nothing would grow until she found her beloved Persephone.

Demeter's search lasted many moons. In her misery she grew old and grey, until at last one day she met a swineherd who had seen Hades abduct Persephone. Her great sadness then turned to anger. Demeter hurried to Zeus and demanded that he command Hades to give Persephone back. Without her daughter, Demeter would never be able to give her blessings to the earth again. Zeus could not let the entire world turn cold and die, so he ordered Hades to send Persephone back to her mother. Hades knew better than to defy Zeus. So he released Persephone.

The reunion of mother and daughter was a beautiful sight. The entire world celebrated. Persephone skipped once more and flowers sprang up wherever her feet touched the earth. And Demeter was once again a radiant and beautiful goddess blessing the bountiful land. All throughout the land grain and fruit grew in abundance.

However, during her long wait, Persephone had forgotten the warning about not eating in the realm of the dead. She had mindlessly tasted six of the sweet seeds from the pomegranate fruit. When Zeus rescued her, Hades demanded justice for the fruit that she had eaten and Persephone realised that she would have to return to his realm. Zeus, in his fairness, decided that Persephone would spend one month in the underworld for each of the seeds she had eaten. Every year she would spend six months with Hades, and the other six with her mother Demeter.

And so, every year when Persephone goes down to be queen in the realm of Hades, Demeter grieves and nothing grows. It is winter on earth. When Persephone returns six months later, all the earth bursts into bloom. It is spring. Mother and daughter rejoice and the fields are fertile once more. So progresses the cycle of the seasons on earth.

Demeter, however, is a loving goddess and does not like to see the people suffering during the cold winter months. So she scattered her golden grain over all the fertile lands and taught people how to tend it, to sow it in the spring and to reap it in the autumn. Then she showed them how to grind it and knead it into dough. And lastly, she taught them how to bake it with fire into tasty loaves of bread so that they would have plenty to eat throughout the entire year.

The king's loaves
Folktale from Afghanistan

There were two beggars, one poorer than the next, who went each day to the gate of the king's palace to beg for food. And every day after the king had eaten his lunch, his servant would bring a loaf of bread for each of them. One of the beggars would always praise the king for his kindness and generosity. But the other offered his praises to God, thanking God that the king should have such wealth that he could give charity to the poor.

The second beggar's words always hurt the king's pride. So the king decided to teach him a lesson. The king ordered his baker to bake two identical loaves of bread. Inside one he had the baker conceal precious jewels. Then the king instructed the baker to give this loaf with the hidden jewels to the beggar who always thanked the king himself for his charity. The plain loaf should go to the second beggar, who thanked God.

And so the next day the baker went to the palace gate and handed the two loaves to the two beggars. The baker was careful not to confuse the two, for he feared the king's wrath should he make a mistake.

The first beggar, who had been given the special, jewel-filled loaf, noticed how heavy and hard his loaf was. He concluded that it was poorly made. Hoping to get the best loaf for himself, he asked the other beggar if he would be willing to exchange loaves with him. The second beggar, always eager to help a friend, agreed. They traded loaves and went their separate ways.

When the second man sat down and bit into his loaf, he was astonished to find that it was filled with precious jewels. He knelt down, and with tears in his eyes thanked God for his good fortune. Now he would never have to beg for his bread again.

The next day only the first beggar came to the palace gate. The king was furious. He called for the baker to be brought before him and asked, 'Did you mix up the two loaves I had you bake?"

'No, your majesty,' answered the trembling baker. 'I did just as you had commanded.'

Then the king turned to the beggar and asked, 'What did you do with the loaf you received yesterday?'

The man replied, 'It was hard and poorly baked. I gave it to my friend in exchange for his.'

The king paused and stroked his long white beard in silence.

Gradually his face lightened as he began to understand how the loaves had been exchanged. It was now clear to him that all his riches had indeed come from God. Only the Holy One, he realised, could make a poor man rich or a rich man poor. Not even a king could change the will of heaven.

The greedy baker
A Sufi wisdom tale

In the old bazaar by the wall of the great mosque stood a small bakery. It was nothing special to look at, but the smell of the fresh baked bread and sweet pastries was delicious. These aromas spread throughout the bazaar. They smelled so good that many people would wander by just to enjoy the tempting scents of the delicacies being offered. Sometimes even crowds blocked the alleyway to savour the delicious smells coming from the bakery.

Well, the baker was a businessman, who cared more for coppers than for company. When he discovered that more people were enjoying the smell of his bread than were buying it from his shop, he complained bitterly to the sultan. But the sultan would do nothing. So, the baker decided to take matters into his own hands. But as so often happens, this soon led to other problems.

The very next day a poor man paused by the bakery, breathed deeply and smiled as the smell of fresh bread filled his senses. The baker charged out in a cloud of flour, and demanded that he be paid at once. Shocked by this unreasonable demand, the poor man was unwilling to part with any of his coins. They began to argue loudly.

Drawn by the sound of this argument the wisest mullah in all the land came to see if he could settle things fairly. He listened carefully to the whole story and then asked the baker, 'How much is a loaf of bread worth?'

'Three copper coins,' answered the baker with outstretched palm.

The mullah then listened to the poor man who told him that the smell of the baking bread travelled far and wide for anyone to enjoy. In fact, he could not help but to smell this bread from the other side of the bazaar.

The wise mullah closed his eyes in thought, stroked his long beard and then proclaimed, 'Goods enjoyed must be paid for! You, poor man, present me with your purse.'

With tears in his eyes, the poor man handed the little purse containing his money to the mullah. The mullah took three copper coins from the man's purse and called the baker beside him.

'Listen,' he commanded. Then he dropped the coins one by one onto the counter. 'Do you recognise the sound? Is it good money?' 'It is,' replied the baker.

'Well then! You have been paid in full,' decreed the wise mullah. 'For the pleasure of the smell of your fresh bread, you have the right to listen to the sound of his good money.'

Then all was fair and right.

Rice is gold
Folktale from India

Long, long ago during the Indian festival of Dassera, a king rode through his city on the back of a great elephant. On that day he greeted his subjects and showered them with many gifts. The streets were decorated in all the bright colours of the sunrise to honour the king. Many people rich and poor lined up along the streets hoping to get food and blessings and gifts from him.

Along one of the roads, a beggar said to himself, 'Today is my lucky day. I shall get plenty to eat. And, if I happen to get near to the king, I may even get some gold. Then I will not need to beg for my living ever again.' With trembling heart, the beggar waited anxiously for the king to pass by.

After some time, the king's parade arrived and there was the king atop his elephant, which was covered in rich cloths and had a saddle studded with gold and gems.

The crowd instantly rushed forward to be nearer to their king. The beggar too pushed forward with his begging bowl that had a handful of rice in it.

'My bowl, your honour! My bowl!' cried the beggar to attract the attention of the king. 'My bowl. I am poor. Give me some alms.'

The king looked down at him with compassion in his eyes. Then he said, 'First, you give me something.'

The beggar felt cheated and annoyed. What could he give? He threw a single grain of rice at the king in disgust. The king in return dropped something in the beggar's bowl and rode away. The beggar grabbed it. It was a piece of gold as big as a single grain of rice.

'I am nothing but a selfish fool,' cried the beggar. 'Why did I not give the king all of my rice?'

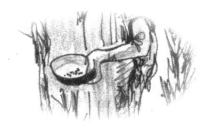

Chapter Three

Tips and ingredients

'The gift of a loaf of bread is one of the heart's dearest currencies – giving the gift of nourishment far surpasses the gathered, stirred, formed and warmed grain. It is the intent to create, through the alchemy of goodwill, as much as through the heat of the fire, that which will sustain another, in body as well as soul. The gift of a loaf of bread is a treasure indeed, whose taste and sweet scent lingers and satisfies, long after the last crumb is gone. I still remember it – whole wheat with cranberries – yum.'

Thank you note from a friend

Starting to knead

Here comes the fun bit. Time to roll up your sleeves and get your hands into the living bread dough. It is good exercise, and everyone can join in. First, wash your hands. Remove any watches, bracelets or rings so they do not become encrusted in dough – or worse yet, a part of the actual loaves. Tie your hair back (if you have any) and put on an apron to protect your clothes.

Choose a recipe and make sure that you have all the ingredients on hand. Once you have added all the ingredients from your bread recipe into the bowl, it will become harder and harder to stir. When it gets too difficult for you or your spoon, sprinkle some flour onto a work surface to keep things from sticking and empty the entire contents of the mixing bowl onto the work surface. Scrape the sides of the bowl with a flexible scraper so that nothing is wasted. Then, work with both hands to incorporate all the ingredients into one uniform blob of dough.

How to knead

Kneading is a process of stretching and folding until the dough becomes smooth and elastic. At first the ingredients look lumpy, sticky and completely unwieldy but with every kneading stroke the dough gets firmer, more consistent and stretchy. Kneading is best done with the heels of both palms in a rhythmic manner. You press with your left hand and fold the dough back in half with your right hand. Then press with your right hand and fold the dough in half with your left, back and forth, in a figure of eight motion. Try to keep your arms straight and let the weight of your body do the work. In a few minutes you will feel the consistency of the dough change as it springs to life.

Work gently with your dough, never roughly. I encourage bakers to press down dough rather than punch it down, as is often suggested in recipes. Punching gives the wrong impression to children (and the dough!). It is much better to treat it kindly and press the air from it before shaping it into loaves.

If the dough is sticking to your hands or to the surface, sprinkle on more flour and knead it in. If the dough feels too stiff, press your fingers in the middle to make a small indentation, then add several drops of water and knead it in. Your aim is dough that feels smooth, elastic and pliable.

Is the dough ready?

The lift of bread increases with kneading, so do not skimp. Usually 10 minutes of vigorous kneading is enough. You know it's done when it becomes one uniform mass that no longer sticks to the table. All the flour has been fully incorporated and the dough feels smooth and uniform. You can test it by pressing a finger into it. If the dough bounces back, the dough is done. If it leaves an impression then carry on. It is nearly impossible to over-knead bread dough by hand (not so with a machine which can tear the delicate protein fibres apart), so keep at it for 10 minutes. Add an extra five minutes when using whole wheat and other grains. These take longer to break down and build a strong gluten network. Soon your hands will know the right consistency.

Baker's attitude

Kneading bread dough can be an energetic workout, or relaxing. You choose what suits your mood – and that of the dough. Keep in mind that your hands are literally caressing every molecule of the bread dough. If it were sensitive to what you are thinking and feeling, which I believe it is, then this is a perfect time to relax, recall something that fills you with joy, sing a song or recite a prayer. The energy you create will be absorbed by the developing bread dough and baked right into the final loaves.

'Giving the hands rhythmic exercises also settles the mind. Many a housewife over the generations has released her frustration and fury as she comes to terms with things during the contained process of kneading bread! I still hear of this today.'

An experienced bread baker and teacher

It is fine to make a mess so dress comfortably. Why not wear an apron and a chef's hat? Children enjoy dressing the part and it makes the activity extra special.

Children will not need to be coerced into baking. Once they see adults interested and involved up to their elbows, they will naturally want to join in the fun. Let them enter slowly at their own pace. Then, like a fine leaven, the good impressions and tastes will nourish them for years to come.

Tips on storing bread

Hard work and anticipation make it so tempting to eat bread fresh from the oven, but it is better if you wait at least 20 minutes for it to complete its baking after being taken out of the oven.

If you do not devour all of the bread that day, keep it unwrapped in a wooden bread box for the first three days. A paper or cloth sack will do as well. After three days, I wrap the loaves in plastic to preserve their moisture. Often they keep this way for over a week. Be careful not to put them in plastic too soon as the moisture will cause them to go mouldy.

If your loaves of bread are beginning to dry out, moisten them with water by briefly turning on the tap. Then warm the loaves in the oven at medium

heat for 10 minutes. Or cut and moisten individual slices, then warm them in the toaster. The steam from the water will soften the crust and enliven the bread.

Baking with a busy schedule

Many of us are just too busy to carve out three hours every week to bake bread from start to finish. That's fine! Instead, put aside three hours every few months to bake a batch. Extra loaves can be frozen until needed.

Make sure to let them cool completely and then wrap them well in airtight plastic. They keep well in the freezer for up to six months. When you want to serve them take them from the freezer, wrap in foil and warm them in an oven at 180°C /350°F/Gas Mark 4 for 15 to 20 minutes.

Never put loaves in the refrigerator as this only accelerates the natural process by which bread goes stale.

If you want individual slices a few at a time, then it is best to slice the fresh loaves when they are cooled into individual slices. Wrap these in airtight plastic and freeze them. Take them from the freezer as desired and pop them in the toaster. Either way, frozen bread will taste nearly as good as when it was first baked. Often it is hard to tell the difference.

One mother I know bakes six loaves at a time for her family of four. They devour one immediately. They eat two over the next few days and the other three she slices, wraps in plastic and freezes. She takes out slices as needed and pops these in the toaster, feeling proud she can feed her family home-baked bread.

Natural breaks – when to interrupt the process

Another strategy for busy bakers involves interrupting the baking process (see example below) and putting the dough in the refrigerator to wait for a day or so until you have more time. Covered, it will keep for up to a day (and up to three days for sourdough). So you can start dough in the evening, put it in the refrigerator and then complete the baking the next day for, say, a special brunch. Or you could prepare the dough in the morning and bake it in the evening for a pizza party. Bread can be flexible to work with your schedule.

1. Mix and knead any bread dough recipe using room temperature water instead of warmer skin temperature. The yeast will take longer to activate when the water is cooler.

2. **Optional stop #1:** Refrigerate dough in covered bowl or a plastic bag for up to 1 day (up to 3 days with sourdough leaven). This slows down but does not completely stop the process of fermentation. (If you wait too long, the bread dough will smell unpleasantly alcoholic. It has become too mature and needs to be composted.)

3. Take dough out of the refrigerator and let it warm for 30 minutes. The culture will become more active and the dough quite springy. It is much nicer to work with warm dough.

4. Shape dough into loaves and place in tins.

5. **Optional stop #2:** Wrap tins in plastic bags/film and refrigerate for up to 4 hours (up to 24 hours for sourdough leaven). This step is called 'retardation' and is used by many artisan bakeries to get lighter and even more flavourful loaves of bread.

6. Take the loaves out of the refrigerator and let them rise until the original volume has doubled. Bake as instructed.

INGREDIENTS AND EQUIPMENT

Local and organic/biodynamic ingredients

Children, much more than adults, are sensitive to the foods they eat. They have clear likes and dislikes and can at times be frustratingly picky. They are in the process of building organs, growing tissue and bone. You can observe in babies how the sense of taste involves their whole bodies, right down to their toes. If a food agrees with their system, they move in a harmonious and calm manner, as if delighting in the sensation of eating. If foods do not agree, their movements are jerky and filled with tension. Special care needs to be taken to give them wholesome food that does not contain potentially harmful chemicals or additives. Good food gives them the forces to build healthy bodies, balanced social relationships and clear thinking.

When shopping, I like to know that I am getting good quality food. Organic and biodynamic are best, but I want it fresh and to support my local economy as well. So, locally produced organic and biodynamic food is even better. This is how I make my decisions. By buying organic and biodynamic food, I am getting the best nourishment for my family. I am also supporting farms that care for their animals, wildlife and the soil. Buying quality ingredients supports my family's health as well as the health of the earth.

Biodynamic agriculture is the oldest consciously organic approach to farming and gardening. Biodynamic growers aim to foster a healthy and sustainable relationship between plant, animal and human life on their farms or gardens. These are maintained through specially crafted compost and by working with an awareness of the rhythms of growth that also take into account the influence of the movements of the sun, moon and planets on plant growth. Biodynamic farmers produce healthy food and vital soil to keep farms productive for generations.

White flour

I prefer working with whole grains and flours. I like the taste of whole wheat and there is no question it makes a healthier loaf. But it is not always the best choice when working with children. It can be sticky and difficult to handle. Some children, especially if they are not used to it, can resist eating it.

White flour is refined from the whole wheat grain. The healthy outer bran and the inner seed germ are removed, making it lighter and easier to work with. White flour has a useful place when baking with children. It makes a smooth elastic dough that is easier for young hands, making kneading more playful. For older hands, it lends itself to textural variations in creative and festive bread-making.

White flour itself also keeps longer than whole wheat flour without spoiling, because there is no oily seed germ to go rancid. Sometimes white flour is bleached and/or fortified with vitamins to compensate for those lost in the refinement process. This is not the case with organic and biodynamic flours. These are neither bleached nor treated with fungicides or other chemicals. If you cannot find organic flour, then it is best to use unbleached white flour.

The two main types of white bread flour

Strong flour is made from high protein (gluten) wheat and is also called bread flour, hard wheat or winter wheat. It forms strong elastic dough that rises beautifully. It will make the lightest and airiest bread.

Plain flour has less gluten and is commonly called cake flour, pastry flour or soft flour. Its structure is more delicate and crumbly. It is not as well suited to making bread. There are also other varieties (and close relatives) of wheat flour (semolina, durum, spelt, kamut, emmer and einkorn) that can be a tasty addition to bread. These are discussed in the chapter on the seven grains 'Seven grains and nutrition'.

Whole wheat (wholemeal)

Children who are picky eaters take time before they are open to eating whole grain breads. Baking is an opportunity to introduce them to new tastes and textures. If they see you enjoying an unusual food and not making a big deal about it, they are more likely to try some too. I have made the whole grain recipes as simple and child-friendly as possible.

Read food labels carefully as they can be deceptive. Only stone ground whole wheat has all the nutrition of the original wheat. The heat of modern roller milling can denature these fragile compounds. Also, once roller milled, 'whole wheat flour' may in fact be reconstituted from white flour (possibly bleached) with some bran and germ added back in. Some wholemeal flour sold in the UK actually has only 85 percent of the whole wheat. The germ has been removed to prevent spoilage. Unfortunately this also removes many of the vitamins and minerals.

You can replace white flour with up to half (50 percent) whole wheat flour. It makes the recipes both more nutritious and more substantial. The dough will be a bit heavier and stickier, so extend kneading times by five minutes to allow the gluten to fully develop. This will help lighten the loaves. A well- kneaded wholemeal loaf can be wonderfully airy with a marvellous crust.

Other flours
You can use up to one quarter (25 percent) of any other grain flour in any of the recipes to add flavour and texture. Try using rye, rice, oat, millet, barley, amaranth, quinoa or maize (corn) flours. You can also use flours made from beans such as pinto,

chickpea or lentils. Keep in mind that only wheat and rye have the proteins necessary to hold the bread together and thus to trap the air that helps it to rise. Other grains will make your bread a little more dense and crumbly.

Have some extra flour on hand, at least 100g (1 cup) when baking bread to keep the dough from sticking to your hands or the counter. It is also helpful in cleaning up mixing spoons and bowls. Simply sprinkle on some flour and rub off any last bits of dough.

Added ingredients
You can include cooked, soaked or sprouted grains to a bread recipe. These add nutrition, flavour and texture but do not help the bread to rise. Add up to a cup of cooked or sprouted grain to each loaf. Bread is also an ideal way to use up extra porridge or rice. I have successfully used leftover pasta kneaded right into the dough – surprisingly tasty! As long as most of the flour is wheat or rye, there will be enough gluten to hold the loaves together. They will work.

DIFFERENT WAYS TO MAKE BREAD RISE

My recipes include quick breads, long ripening sourdoughs and yeasted breads. They all use different ways to make the bread rise. Quick breads employ chemical rising agents, such as bicarbonate of soda (baking soda) and baking powder. This type can be made from start to finish in less than an hour.

In contrast, the process for creating and ripening your own sourdough starter takes two weeks. However, once made, the same leaven can be used to bake delicious breads for years. It can even be passed down to future generations for their baking. Traditionally, bakers treated their leaven as a precious family heirloom. It is what gave their bread its unique quality and flavour. There is more about sourdough later in this chapter (see 'Making a sourdough culture', page 109).

Recipes using yeast (fresh or dried) take about three hours from start to finish.

Yeast

The word 'yeast' comes from the Sanskrit 'yas', meaning to seethe or boil. Yeast are used in baking bread, brewing beer, wine and vinegar. Yeast naturally abound in the air, water and earth around us. They are common single-celled living organisms from the fungus family, which make their living breaking down other organisms. Baker's yeast as well as brewer's yeast belong to the Saccharomyces cerevisiae species. In fact, this is why traditionally bakeries and breweries were located in proximity to one another, so that they could share their yeast.

Our understanding of yeast's role in the process of fermentation is credited to Louis Pasteur whose experiments in the 1850s led to the development of today's baking yeast. Simply put, yeast cells feed on the sugars in flour and convert these into carbon dioxide and alcohol. The carbon dioxide is then trapped by the balloon-like layers of gluten, which literally inflate and make the bread rise. If bread is allowed to rise for too long, the structure becomes over-inflated and fragile. Also, the levels of alcohol in the dough rise to the point that the taste is quite unpleasant.

Dried and fresh yeast

You can buy yeast in either dried or fresh form. In most recipes they can be used interchangeably as they have similar working qualities and flavour. To convert a recipe use the following amounts:

1 cube of fresh yeast = 15g (1 tbsp) dried yeast.

It takes about three hours using dried or fresh yeast for the dough to rise and be ready to bake.

I discourage the use of 'quick-acting' (or 'rapid rise') yeast because I do not like its working qualities or taste. Flavour has been sacrificed for speed. The bread dough has little time to develop its own natural flavours or nutritive value. Besides, it is easier to make catastrophic mistakes with quick-acting yeast because it rises so quickly. The dough easily becomes over-ripe, fragile and alcoholic. The working window has been narrowed and the bread will not easily recover from any neglect if you are not ready to bake it there and then.

Whether fresh, dried or quick-acting, commercial yeast is a monoculture of highly refined and purified yeast that is engineered to work quickly.

Water

Commercial yeast requires warm water to grow and multiply. Generally speaking, the ideal temperature is body temperature, comfortable to take a bath in but not as hot as a cup of tea. If you are using a thermometer, yeast develops best in water between 32°C and 38°C (90°F and 100°F). Any cooler, and the yeast will grow very slowly. Temperatures above 58°C (138°F) will kill the yeast. This is why I suggest starting the yeast with some sugar (or flour if not using sugar) in warm water. Then you can make sure that the yeast is active and forms a bubbly starter.

Quick no-yeast bread

I have also included recipes for quick breads. These use a chemical rising agent, such as bicarbonate of soda (baking soda) and baking powder and can be made from start to finish in less than an hour. Baking soda bubbles when it is mixed with an acid (such as lemon juice, vinegar or yoghurt). This causes these quick breads to rise and gives them a characteristic tangy taste.

Baking powder works on its own without any additional acids. There are many formulations for baking powder. These can include part baking soda and part cream of tartar, calcium phosphate, calcium citrate and calcium aluminium phosphate. There are some health concerns about eating too much aluminium, so choose carefully.

Sourdoughs

Sourdough is bread made with a homemade yeast, called a sourdough culture, leaven or starter. A sourdough leaven makes the most forgiving, nutritious and flavourful bread. It is well worth experimenting, as sourdough has many advantages for the home baker over yeast or chemical rising agents.

Sourdough bread is easy to digest because the process of breaking down the flour has already begun before you eat it. Yeasts and lactobacilli already present on the grain and in the air create a living community in the starter culture, which is made from just flour and water. These organisms start breaking down the wheat, and also give off carbon dioxide that will cause the dough to rise.

Sourdough's history dates back to ancient Egypt and the first leavened breads. Called 'levain' in France and 'la madre' in Spain, there are as many approaches to sourdough leaven as there are sourdough-eating communities. Bakers through the ages valued their leaven as a close-kept secret. A family heirloom, it was passed down from one generation to the next to give their bread its own unique texture and taste.

Despite sourdough's mystique, you can make your own easily. All you need is flour, water and a little patience. Ripening your starter takes about two weeks. It can then be used to bake delicious breads for years to come. After each baking session you

Sourdough – its benefits

- *Sourdough makes nutrients of the flour bio-available for your digestion and absorption.*
- *The slow rising time allows more flavours to develop in the dough.*
- *Sourdough breaks down components in dough that can be harmful and cause allergic responses in some people.*
- *Sourdough helps the bread to keep fresh longer without spoiling.*

I prefer ingredients in their most natural raw forms, as they are more easily digested. There are many such sugars including demerara, muscovado, turbinado, rapidura, molasses, barley malt, rice syrup, maple syrup and honey. In all of these recipes the sweetener can be interchanged for your preferred one. If you choose to use a liquid sweetener such as honey, you may have to add a little more flour to compensate for the added moisture.

Do not use artificial sweeteners! Formulated in a laboratory, they are not really food, and research shows that some, like aspartame, carry health risks.

simply take out a small ball of the bread dough which contains enough of the original starter (sourdough 'chef') to make your next batch of bread rise. Each loaf is directly related to the ones you baked before, a long lineage of bread. The starter will keep on working for you (and your children and grandchildren) as long as you keep a bit of dough from one session to the next.

It's possible to make a wheat-free starter using rye or spelt. If you are baking for wheat-sensitive people, then make sure your starter is made entirely from rye or spelt flour. These can be developed in exactly the same ways and work beautifully.

Sugar

Natural sugar is listed in many of the recipes but can be reduced or omitted completely according to your dietary preferences. You don't even need sugar to get the yeast started. Simply feed fresh or dried yeast with a bit of flour in warm water to give it a good start. It takes a bit longer than with sugar but it works equally well.

Equipment

- large mixing bowl
- wooden spoon
- measuring scale, cups and spoons
- bread tins or trays
- apron

And of course, an oven

Have ready

- clean countertop, work surface or table, best at belly button height
- sink for washing hands and dishes, sponge and soap
- plastic wrap
- dustpan and brush

Additional aids depending on recipe

- rolling pin
- metal grater
- sharp knife
- juicer
- cooling rack
- pastry knife
- flexible scraper
- pastry brush
- assortment of smaller bowls
- jars to store frequently used ingredients

Ovens and shelves

All types of ovens will bake bread including gas, convection, wood-fired, electric, and even a small table-top oven. Each, however, cooks at a slightly different temperature, and some can vary a lot. If you are unsure about your oven, an oven thermometer comes in handy. Microwave ovens can be interesting for experiments, but produce inedible bread.

Generally it is best to bake on the centre or above centre shelf. This gives optimum heat and circulation in most ovens. If your oven tends to cook unevenly, then rotate the loaves half way through their baking. And if you are baking on more than one shelf, swap the loaves around after half an hour to ensure even cooking.

Bread machines

Bread machines are wonderful because they can introduce people to the basics of baking bread and make it easy to enter the process. They produce fresh baked bread just when it is wanted, even first thing in the morning, filling a home with delicious smells. They have opened the doors for hours of pleasure, experimentation and delicious bread. But, they have their limits too.

As often happens, people's curiosity soon outgrows the capacities of the machine itself. Bread machines do not deal well with whole grain, chunky or sourdough breads. Also there is little possibility for creating chewy or crispy crust or loaf shapes other than cylinders with holes in the middle.

Grain grinders

When possible, I like to grind my grain freshly from whole wheat berries. This assures that I am using the freshest and most nutritious flour. Grinders are available in either hand powered or electric versions. While it can be fun to hand-grind with children, and is truly good work, grinding enough for a few loaves is a considerable amount of work. Thus, an electrical grinder can come in handy. Some look quite attractive on the countertop.

Work surfaces

The height is important as it helps to make your kneading efficient. A countertop at waist to belly button height is ideal. Adults and children tend to work at different heights. If the surface is too high for children, let them stand on a telephone book or a chair so that they can be fully part of the process. Its surface can be made from wood, metal, formica or tile as long as it is easy to clean.

Conversion chart

I have attempted to make all recipes in this book easy to follow whether you live in Europe, the UK or the United States of America. All measurements are given in metric and imperial/US as well as in both weight and volume for flour. Avoid switching between the two systems as some of them have been rounded up or down in order to keep the proportions accurate for the recipes. There is a great variation in ingredients, their moisture content and their handling properties. Some adjustments may need to be made in your kitchen.

Abbreviations

tsp = teaspoon	tbsp = tablespoon
oz = ounce	fl oz = fluid ounce
lb = pound	in = inch
kg = kilogram	g = gram
l = litre	ml = millilitre

°C = degrees Celsius
°F = degrees Fahrenheit

Weight measures

Metric	Imperial
14g	1/2 oz
28g	1 oz
57g	2 oz
227g	8 oz (1/2 lb)
454g	16 oz (1 lb)
1kg	36 oz (2.2 lb)

Liquid measures

Metric	Imperial
5ml	1 tsp
15ml	1 tbsp (½ fl oz)
30ml	1 fl oz
60ml	2 fl oz
237ml	8 fl oz (1 cup)
473ml	16 fl oz (2 cups)
591ml	20 fl oz (1 British pint)
1litre	34 fl oz

Oven temperatures

°C	°F	Gas Mark
110	225	¼
120	250	½
140	275	1
150	300	2
170	325	3
180	350	4
190	375	5
200	400	6
220	425	7
230	450	8
240	475	9

Chapter Four

Recipes

Many of these recipes involve handling very hot oil or water and hot ovens, so careful adult supervision is required.

FUN BREADS

Easy white bread

This simple white bread (and children love simple food) serves as the foundation for many of the creative bread recipes to come. Make this yeasted dough side by side with children, and learn together how it feels. You can expand your creative bread baking by adding to or varying the basic ingredients.

Ingredients for 2 large loaves

METRIC	IMPERIAL/US	
1 kg	2lbs (8 cups)	strong flour (hard wheat, winter wheat or bread flour)
100g	4oz (1 cup)	extra flour, as needed to keep dough from sticking
25g	2 tbsp	natural sugar
24g	2 tsp	sea salt
10g	1 tbsp	dried yeast (not 'quick acting')
600ml	21fl oz (2½ cups)	warm water (body temperature is best)
30ml	2 tbsp	vegetable oil

1. In a large bowl, dissolve yeast in warm water with sugar. Let the liquid rest in a warm place for 10 minutes, until it is bubbly and smells yeasty. If the water is too hot (above 50°C /120°F) this will kill the yeast. If it is below 26°C /80°F everything will proceed very slowly.

2. Mix the salt into the yeast and slowly add this to the flour until it comes together into a blob. The dough should still be soft and slightly sticky to the touch.

3. Sprinkle some flour onto a clean work surface (the right height is between waist and navel). Knead the dough, folding in the loose flour until the dough is elastic but does not stick to your hands or the counter. It is better to start with dough that is too wet and add flour than to have it be too dry and have to add more water, although that too can be done. Knead with vigour for 10 minutes. This is the perfect time to sing a bread song or to knead a blessing right into the dough.

4. Grease a large bowl with vegetable oil. Place the dough in the bowl and cover with a moist tea towel or with plastic wrap to keep in moisture. Let the dough rise in a warm place for 1½ hours until it doubles in volume.

5. Press the dough down to release extra gas. Punching down the dough gives the wrong impression to children. It is much better to treat it gently and to press the air from it. Then cut the dough in half and shape into loaves by stretching and folding the dough so that it has a nice taut skin on top without any creases. Place in greased baking tins with any seams on the underside. Let it rise again until the volume doubles, about ½ hour.

6. Bake in preheated oven at 200°C/400°F/Gas Mark 6 for 30 to 40 minutes or until golden brown. The underside will give a hollow, wooden sound when tapped with a finger.

7. Let bread cool for 20 minutes before slicing. This completes the baking process and improves the final texture.

Variations
*   Add a handful of raisins or sunflower seeds (approx 100g /4 oz / 1⁄2 cup)
*   Shape as individual dinner rolls:
    *   cut dough into 16 pieces
    *   let children shape their own rolls
    *   place on a greased baking sheet
    *   bake in preheated oven for 20 to 25 minutes or until golden brown

I received this advice from an avid home baker and kindergarten teacher:
'The whole process of baking bread is transformative. New children enter slowly into the experience. At first they can be finicky, hesitant to touch this strange, sticky dough. Giving them a bowl of flour to dip their hands into first helps the dough be less sticky. But soon their joy of working with it grows until they are completely absorbed in the activity of kneading and creating loaves of bread.'

Grandma's split top wheat bread

Wholemeal bread provides good nutrition for growing children. Here is another easy recipe with which to develop skill and confidence by baking this everyday staple bread, adding to or varying the basic ingredients.

Ingredients for 2 large loaves

METRIC	IMPERIAL/US	
500g	1lb (4 cups)	strong flour (hard wheat, winter wheat or bread flour)
100g	4oz (1 cup)	extra flour, as needed to keep dough from sticking
500g	1lb (4 cups)	strong white flour
30ml	2 tbsp	honey
24g	2 tsp	sea salt
7g	1 flat tbsp	dried yeast (not 'quick acting')
600ml	21fl oz (2½ cups)	warm water (body temperature is best)
30ml	2 tbsp	vegetable oil

1. In a large bowl, dissolve yeast in warm water with honey. Let the liquid rest in a warm place for 10 minutes, until it is bubbly and smells yeasty. If the water is too hot (above 50°C/120°F) this will kill the yeast. If it is too cold everything will proceed very slowly.

2. Mix in salt and slowly add the flour until it comes together into a blob. The dough should still be soft and slightly sticky to the touch.

3. Sprinkle some flour onto a clean work surface that stands between waist and navel height. Knead the dough, folding in loose flour so that the dough is elastic but does not stick to your hands or the counter. It is better to start with dough that is too wet and to add flour than to have it be too dry and to have to add more water, although that too can be done. Knead with vigour for 10 minutes. This is the perfect time to sing a bread song or to knead a blessing right into the dough.

4. Grease a large bowl with vegetable oil. Place the dough in the bowl and cover with a moist tea towel or with plastic wrap to keep in moisture. Let the dough rise in a warm place for 1½ hours until it doubles in volume.

5. Press the dough down to release extra gas. Punching down the dough gives the wrong impression to children. It is much better to treat it gently and to press the air from it. Then cut the dough in half and shape into loaves by stretching and folding the dough so that it has a nice taut skin on top without any creases. Place in greased baking tins with any seams on the under- side. Let it rise again until the volume doubles, about ½ hour.

6. Bake in preheated oven at 200°C /400°F/ Gas Mark 6 for 30 to 40 minutes or until golden brown. The underside will give a hollow, wooden sound when tapped with a finger.

7. Let bread cool for 20 minutes before slicing. This completes the baking process and improves the final texture.

Variations
- Use up to 100% whole wheat flour. This makes the kneading a bit more strenuous.
- Add an extra 5 minutes so that the dough will rise nicely.
- Extend rising times if needed to allow the more dense bread to double in volume before cooking.

One year a father made a new dollhouse for our kindergarten. We decided to have an opening ceremony for which everyone would make something for the new house. We baked tiny doll-sized loaves of our favourite bread, cut them in slices and spread them with butter and honey. We made special plates for each of the dolls and served them with the tiny honey sandwiches along with tea in dolls' cups at the opening ceremony. Baking made the doll- house feel like home, so it was truly ours.

Oatmeal apple raisin bread

This bread evokes the warm flavour of home cooked cinnamon apple oatmeal. It is slightly sweet and moist, and wonderful as part of a healthy breakfast.

Ingredients for 2 large loaves

METRIC	IMPERIAL/US	
800g	1lb 8 oz (6½ cups)	strong white flour
225g	10 oz (3 cups)	rolled oats (porridge oats)
20g	2 tbsp	natural sugar or honey
24g	2 tsp	sea salt
10g	1 tbsp	dried yeast (not 'quick acting')
600ml	21 fl oz (2½ cups)	warm water (body temperature is best)
30ml	2 tbsp	vegetable oil
173g	6 oz (1cup)	raisins
		1 large apple, finely chopped
15g	1 tbsp	cinnamon

1. In a large bowl dissolve yeast in warm water with sugar/honey. Add rolled oats. Let the mixture rest in a warm place for 10 minutes, until the liquid is bubbly and smells yeasty.

2. Mix in apple, raisins, salt, oil and cinnamon. Slowly add the flour until it comes together into a blob. The dough should still be soft and slightly sticky to the touch.

3. Knead the dough for 10 minutes. Apples will make the dough moister as you knead. Add just enough extra flour so that the dough stays elastic but not too sticky.

4. Grease a large bowl with vegetable oil. Place the dough in the bowl and cover with a moist tea towel or with plastic wrap to keep in moisture. Let the dough rise in a warm place for 1½ to 2 hours until it doubles in volume.

5. Cut the dough in half and shape into loaves by stretching and folding the dough. Place in greased baking tins with the seams on the underside. The dough should fill only ⅔ of the tin because it will rise above the rim.

6. Moisten the tops with a little water (sprayed, brushed or rubbed on with your hand). Sprinkle rolled oats on top for the classic look. Let it rise again until the volume doubles, about ½ hour.

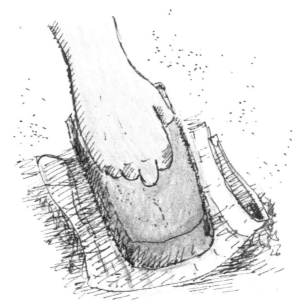

7. Bake in a preheated oven at 190°C /375°F/ Gas Mark 5 for 40 minutes or until golden brown. The underside will give a hollow, wooden sound when tapped with a finger.

Rosemary, rice and rye bread

This wheat-free recipe combines the rich flavour of rye with the crunchy lightness of brown rice flour. Fresh rosemary and lemon zest give it a stunning aroma. This is a no-knead bread that goes straight from the mixing bowl into bread tins, avoiding any extra mess in your kitchen.

Ingredients for 2 small loaves

METRIC	IMPERIAL/US	
400g	14 oz (3½ cups)	rye flour
200g	7 oz (1¾ cups)	brown rice flour
38g	3 tbsp	raw sugar or honey
24g	2 tsp	sea salt
5g	2 tsp	dried yeast (not 'quick acting')
400ml	14 fl oz (1¾ cups)	warm water (body temperature is best)
30ml	2 tbsp	olive oil
5g	2 tbsp	fresh or dried rosemary
10g	1 tbsp	lemon zest (grated rind)

1. In a large bowl, dissolve yeast in warm water with sugar/ honey. Let it sit for 10 minutes until the liquid is bubbly and smells yeasty.

2. Mix in the salt, oil, rosemary and lemon zest. Slowly stir in the flour using a wooden spoon or your bare hands until it all comes together in a moist and sticky dough. Stir with vigour for 5 minutes, making sure there are no lumps. This is the perfect time to sing a bread song or to stir a blessing right into the dough.

3. Keep the dough in the bowl and let it rise in a warm place for 1½ hours until doubled in volume.

4. Grease two 1lb (small) loaf bread tins. Smaller tins allow the inside of this moist bread to fully cook. Spoon the still sticky dough into them. Then use a wet spoon to smooth the tops of the loaves. Allow the loaves to rise in a warm place for 1 hour or until they double in volume. Warmer temperatures make all the steps happen more quickly. You will have to experiment to see what works best in your kitchen.

5. Bake the loaves in a preheated oven at 180°C/350°F/Gas Mark 4 for 40 minutes or until done.

6. Let bread cool for 20 minutes before slicing. It is still cooking with its own steam on the inside.

Millet poppy birdseed bread

'There is bread and then there is bread!' as a friend once said to me after tasting this loaf. This rich seedy bread is not for the birds though they will love it too. It takes a bit more effort in the kneading, but the crunchy result with a hint of lemon is well worth it.

Ingredients for 2 large loaves

METRIC	IMPERIAL/US	
500g	1 lb (4 cups)	strong white flour
400g	14 oz (3½ cups)	spelt flour
300g	10 oz (2½ cups	millet (whole grain)
50g	4 tbsp	raw sugar or honey
18g	1 tbsp	sea salt
10g	1 tbsp	dried yeast (not 'quick acting')
600ml	21 fl oz (2½ cups)	warm water (body temperature is best)
125ml	4 fl oz (½ cup)	juice of 2 lemons
20g	2 tbsp	lemon zest (grated rind from 1 lemon)
30ml	2 tbsp	vegetable oil
160g	5½ oz (1 cup)	poppy seeds
125g	4½ oz (½ cup)	sunflower seeds
125g	4½ oz (½ cup)	pumpkin seeds

1. In a large bowl, dissolve yeast in warm water with sugar/honey and millet seeds. Let it rest in a warm place for 10 minutes, until the liquid is bubbly and smells yeasty.

2. Mix in all other seeds, salt, oil, lemon juice and zest. Then slowly add the flours until everything comes together in a blob. This dough will be dense and slightly sticky to the touch. Don't add any more flour than is necessary to keep it from sticking.

3. Knead with vigour for 10 minutes. This is my favourite time to knead a blessing and thankfulness right into the dough.

4. Grease a large bowl with vegetable oil. Place the dough in the bowl and cover with a moist tea towel or plastic wrap to keep in moisture. Let the dough rise in a warm place for 1½ to 2 hours until it doubles in volume.

5. Cut the dough in half and shape into loaves by stretching and folding the dough. Place in greased baking tins with the seams on the underside. Let it rise again until the volume doubles, about 1/2 hour.

6. Bake in a preheated oven at 190°C /375°F/ Gas Mark 5 for 40 minutes or until golden brown. The underside will give a hollow, wooden sound when tapped with a finger.

7. Cool for 20 minutes. The seeds you've baked right in will be revealed with each slice. Make sure to save all the crumbs for hungry birds or bake a tiny loaf just for them.

Thursday was baking day, as the children called it. When they came to school in the morning, they would find their little aprons hung on the backs of their chairs, all ready for baking. They regularly greeted me with cheers of delight, 'Oh! It's baking day!' It was the most popular day of the week.

Roman army bread

Coarse barley bread was the food of common people from the times of ancient Egypt through to the Roman empire. Spelt, an older cousin of wheat, was also eaten in Roman times. It is flavourful and sustaining over the long haul. This modern wheat-free recipe includes honey and sunflower seeds for extra energy and nutrition. After all, 'an army only marches as far as its stomach will carry it.'

Ingredients for 2 large loaves

METRIC	IMPERIAL/US	
500g	1lb (4 cups)	spelt flour
200g	8oz (2 cups)	rolled barley or barley flour
24g	2 tsp	sea salt
10g	1 tbsp	dried yeast (not 'quick acting')
500ml	16fl oz (2 cups)	warm water (body temperature is best)
30ml	2 tbsp	vegetable oil
125ml	4 fl oz (½ cup)	honey
125g	4½ oz (½ cup)	sunflower seeds

1. In a large bowl, dissolve yeast in warm water with honey. Stir in the barley. Let the liquid rest in a warm place for 10 minutes, until it is bubbly and smells yeasty.

2. Stir in salt, oil and sunflower seeds. Slowly add the spelt flour until everything comes together into a sticky blob. The dough should still be soft and slightly moist to the touch.

3. Knead for 10 minutes. This dough tends to be more sticky than others. Try not to add any more flour than is absolutely necessary to keep the dough from sticking to your hands or table top. More flour will make the loaves more dense.

4. Grease a large bowl with vegetable oil. Place the dough in the bowl and cover with a moist tea towel or plastic wrap to keep in the moisture. Let the dough rise in a warm place for 1½ to 2 hours until it doubles in volume. This is a perfect time to learn more about life in ancient Rome.

5. Cut the dough in half and shape into two oval loaves by stretching and folding the dough. Shape until the tops are smooth and free of creases. Place on greased baking trays with any seams on the underside. Sprinkle rolled barley or seeds on the top for an authentic look. Let it rise again until the volume doubles, about 1 hour.

6. Bake in a preheated oven at 190°C /375°F/ Gas Mark 5 for 40 minutes or until brown. These loaves will naturally be a dark brown colour. Test the loaves to see if they are done, by tapping the underside with your finger. They should give a hollow, wooden sound.

7. Let bread cool completely before serving to the masses.

A young teacher recently shared with me: 'My first loaves were like rocks and I was embarrassed to show them to the children's parents. They were terrible! So, instead of giving them to the children to take home as gifts for their families, I hid them beneath the sink. Only later I learned that bread needs patience... my patience, to become light and airy.'

Greek pitta bread

Making pitta bread is magic in action. The **pitta** pockets puff up right before your eyes and **are** sure to be greeted with gasps of awe and delight. Once the dough is prepared it can be rolled and baked in a matter of minutes. This is a sure crowd-pleaser.

Ingredients for 12 small pittas

Metric	Imperial/US	
250g	8 oz (2 cups)	strong white flour (hard or bread flour)
250g	8oz (2 cups)	plain flour (soft white or pastry)
12g	1 tbsp	natural sugar or honey
24g	2 tsp	sea salt
5g	2 tsp	dried yeast (not 'quick acting')
300ml	10 fl oz (1½ cups)	warm water (body temperature is best)

1. In a large bowl, dissolve yeast in warm water with sugar / honey. Let the liquid rest in a warm place for 10 minutes, until it is bubbly and smells yeasty.

2. Add salt and then add the flour until the dough comes together into one big blob. It should still be soft and pliable, but not sticky to the touch.

3. Sprinkle flour onto a clean work surface and knead for 10 minutes.

4. Grease a large bowl with vegetable oil. Place the dough in the bowl and cover with a damp tea towel. Let it rise until double in volume, about 1½ to 2 hours.

5. Preheat oven to 220°C /425°F/Gas Mark 7 and place large iron skillet or baking sheet in the oven.

6. Cut dough into 12 mouse sized pieces. Form these into little balls with seams on the

At our annual May Day festival we fire up the wood-fired bread oven. Children line up to make, and devour, their own pitta creations in a matter of minutes. They are completely transfixed watching the little loaves inflate in the fire-lit oven. The pittas often look like they are going to take off, and that is just when they are done.

I give older children the hot pitta right from the oven and let them flip it between their hands, to play 'hot potato' until it has cooled enough to eat. These pittas are so delicious that neither butter nor jam is needed and rarely does a crust go uneaten.

underside. Coat them with flour. Then with a rolling pin, roll these into discs about ½ cm (⅛ in) thick using enough flour to keep the dough from sticking. Now they are ready for baking.

7. Bake one at a time by tossing the rolled- out dough discs into the hot skillet in the oven. This is fun to watch through a glass oven door and takes only a minute or two. Steam is trapped in the middle of the dough causing the pitta to puff up and a pocket to naturally form inside.

A pitta takes 1 to 2 minutes to cook. You know it's done when it has puffed up, then collapsed a little. It should be light golden brown. Remove from skillet with spatula or tongs.

8. Careful, pittas are filled with steam and hot! Let them cool before eating.

Chapatti

This unleavened bread comes from India where it is used instead of a knife and fork to eat delicious dishes as well as scraping plates clean. Like the Mexican tortilla, it has no rising agent and is truly a flat bread.

Chapattis are quick and easy to make. They are best eaten freshly-made, and served in a cloth-lined basket.

Ingredients for 6 chapattis

METRIC	IMPERIAL/US	
250g	8 oz (2 cups)	strong white flour (hard or bread flour)
15ml	1 tbsp	vegetable oil
24g	2 tsp	sea salt
170ml	6 fl oz (¾ cup)	warm water (body temperature is best)

1. Mix together flour, salt, oil and water. Knead until completely mixed, adding flour to keep dough from sticking.

2. Cover with a damp cloth and let sit for 30 minutes (or longer if need be, covered with plastic in the refrigerator).

3. Divide dough into 6 equal pieces.

4. Roll into 20cm/8 in disc using flour to prevent sticking.

5. Heat a large frying pan without oil.

6. Cook chapatti for a few minutes on either side.

7. Wrap chapatti in a cloth to keep warm until serving. Their shared steam will help them to stay soft.

A mother in Japan cooks chapatti with her children: 'I like to make chapatti every Thursday in my in-home kindergarten. I give each child a small ball of dough and let them shape it with their hands or with rolling pins. They set right to work and each makes her own unique shape. We eat these along with homemade vegetable soup. The children are happy to make their own food and eat it readily without any fuss.'

Bagels

How did bagels get their holes? The bagel originated in 1683, when a Jewish baker from Vienna created them as a gift for the King of Poland to celebrate his victory over the Turks that year. Fashioned in the shape of a stirrup, the bagel commemorated the victorious cavalry charge. Thus the name *bagel* originated from the Polish word 'beugal' for stirrup. Bagels are boiled then baked to give them a chewy texture, a soft brown crust and of course, a hole. They are best topped with melted butter and jam or my favourite, cream cheese and smoked salmon.

Ingredients for 12 bagels

Metric	Imperial/US	
500g	1 lb (4 cups)	strong white flour (hard wheat or bread flour)
12g	1 tbsp	natural sugar or honey
24g	2 tsp	sea salt
5g	2 tsp	dried yeast (not 'quick acting')
300ml	10 fl oz (1½ cups)	warm water (body temperature is best)
		1 egg white
20g	2 tbsp	sesame or poppy seeds to sprinkle on top

1. In a large bowl, dissolve yeast in warm water with sugar/honey. Let the liquid rest in a warm place for 10 minutes, until it is bubbly and smells yeasty.

2. Mix in salt and slowly add the flour until the dough comes together into a blob. It should still be soft and slightly sticky to the touch.

3. Sprinkle some flour onto a clean work surface and knead with vigour for 10 minutes.

4. Grease a large bowl with vegetable oil. Place the dough in the bowl and cover with a damp tea towel.

5. Let it rise until double in volume, about 1½ to 2 hours.

6. After the first rising, cut into 12 pieces and shape dough into 12 small balls.

7. Poke your thumb through the centre of the balls and stretch them to create rings. Let rise on a greased sheet for 20 minutes in a warm place.

8. In a 2 litre (4 pint/2 quart) saucepan, bring water to a gentle boil. Add 24g (2 tbsp) sugar to water. Boiling gives bagels their characteristic chewy crust.

9. Boil bagels 2 or 3 at a time for 30 seconds on each side and then drain them on towel. If bagels do not float on the surface of the water, then they need to rise for a bit longer before boiling.

10. Place bagels on baking sheet with corn meal or semolina flour to keep them from sticking. Brush bagels with egg white diluted with 15ml (1 tbsp) water to make the tops shiny. You can sprinkle bagels with sesame seeds, poppy seeds or coarse salt if desired.

11. Bake in a preheated oven at 200°C/ 400°F/ Gas Mark 6 for 20 minutes or until golden brown.

12. Let cool, slice in half and serve.

In my many bread conversations, I have often heard regrets about not having learned to bake bread. One man, now a solar energy engineer, summed it up, 'My father was a farmer. When he baked bread each week, I would linger near the warm oven waiting with delicious anticipation. Nothing tasted better than fresh hot bread with melted butter and honey. It is sad to say, but he never had the time to let me bake too. And now I do not know how to do it.'

Homemade pizza

Little is more satisfying or more filling than home-baked pizza. These pizzas are perfect creative treats for parties. Children enjoy making their own individual pizzas or helping to create large pans for all the guests. No-one will go hungry.

Ingredients for 1 large pan or 4 individual pizzas

METRIC	IMPERIAL/US	
250g	8 oz (2 cups)	strong white flour (hard or bread flour)
250g	8oz (2 cups)	plain flour (soft white or pastry)
12g	1 tbsp	raw sugar or honey
24g	2 tsp	sea salt
5g	2 tsp	dried yeast (not 'quick acting')
385ml	13 fl oz (1½ cups)	warm water (body temperature is best)
45ml	3 tbsp	olive oil
250ml	8 fl oz (1 cup)	tomato sauce or pasta sauce
250g	8oz (2 cups)	mozzarella cheese and Cheddar cheese (a mixture of cheeses is best)

Various toppings, thinly sliced, e.g. fresh tomato, mushrooms, onions, olives…

1. In a large bowl, dissolve yeast in warm water with sugar/honey. Let the liquid rest in a warm place for 10 minutes, until it is bubbly and smells yeasty.

2. Add salt, olive oil and slowly add the flour until the dough comes together into a blob. It should still be soft and slightly sticky to the touch.

3. Sprinkle flour onto a clean work surface and knead for 10 minutes.

4. Grease a large bowl with vegetable oil. Place the dough in the bowl and cover with a damp tea towel. Let it rise until double in volume, about 1½ to 2 hours.

5. Roll all the dough flat or cut into 4 separate pizzas, each 1cm (½ in) thick and place onto a greased baking sheet. Spread the sauce, layer with cheese and then toppings. Let it rise for 15 minutes and bake in a preheated oven at 200°C /400°F/Gas Mark 6 for 20 minutes or until the cheese is bubbly and golden.

6. Slice and cool before eating. A burned mouth ruins the rest of the experience.

Homemade pizza, baked in the wood-fired bread ovens I have built, has become a favourite birthday treat. Usually the host prepares the dough and the basic ingredients, cheese and tomato sauce. The guests are then invited to bring their preferred toppings. This has led to some remarkably creative and unusual pizzas, especially if the guests you invite come from other cultures and bring things like pineapple, chorizo sausage, seaweed or fried crickets.

Philadelphia soft pretzels

This old time favourite from my hometown is as much a delight to make as to eat, excellent for snacks or to accompany meals. Here are instructions for making a traditional pretzel as well as ideas for other creative shapes, including letters, numbers, knots and… Try your hand and see what innovative forms emerge.

Ingredients for 12 soft pretzels

Metric	Imperial/US	
250g	8 oz (2 cups)	strong white flour (hard wheat or bread flour)
250g	8 oz (2 cups)	plain flour (soft or pastry flour)
12g	1 tbsp	natural sugar
24g	2 tsp	sea salt
5g	2 tsp	dried yeast (not 'quick acting')
300ml	10 fl oz (1¼ cups)	warm water (body temperature is best)
		1 egg yolk
35g	2 tbsp	coarse sea salt to sprinkle on top

1. In a large bowl, dissolve yeast in warm water with sugar. Let the liquid rest in a warm place for 10 minutes, until it is bubbly and smells yeasty.

2. Mix in salt and slowly add the flour until the dough comes together into a blob. It should still be soft and slightly sticky to the touch.

3. Sprinkle some flour onto a clean work surface and knead with vigour for 10 minutes. This is a good time to sing a bread song or to knead a blessing right into the dough.

4. Grease a large bowl with vegetable oil. Place the dough in the bowl and cover with a damp tea towel. Let it rise until double in volume, about 1½ to 2 hours.

5. Press down dough and divide into 12 equal pieces. Roll into 30cm (12 in) lengths, about finger thickness. Twist into traditional pretzel shape or try your own variations. Let it rise for 20 minutes on a greased baking sheet.

6. *This step. can be omitted if time and space do not permit.* Authentic pretzels are boiled in water before baking in the oven. This makes them chewy. Bring water in a 2 litre (4 pint/2 quart) saucepan to a boil. Add 24g (2 tbsp) sugar. Drop the pretzels 1 or 2 at a time into the water. They should rise up to the surface in a few seconds. If not, they need to rise a bit longer. Flip them over after 30 seconds for another 30 seconds. Lift them out with a slotted spoon and let them dry briefly on a towel or napkin. Then place them on a greased baking sheet.

7. Paint the tops with egg yolk diluted with 15ml water. Sprinkle on coarse salt or poppy or sesame seeds.

8. Bake in a preheated oven at 200°C /400°F/Gas Mark 6 for 20 minutes. Eat while still warm. These taste wonderful with mustard squeezed or spread on top.

'When I first became a kindergarten teacher I got so scared when I was told I would have to bake bread with the children. It all seemed so complicated, and I feared that it would be a total failure. But, once I got started, I could not believe how simple it was. I guess this apprehension is why so many people buy bread in shops.'

Cinnamon rolls

These sweet treats are fun to make for a special brunch or an after-meal treat. Children enjoy rolling all the ingredients together then watching the rolls swell and grow together in the tray.

Ingredients for 20 small rolls or 12 large rolls

METRIC	IMPERIAL/US	
500g	1 lb (4 cups)	plain flour (soft white or pastry)
30g	2 tbsp	raw sugar or honey
5g	½ tsp	sea salt
10g	1 tbsp	dried yeast (not 'quick acting')
300ml	10 fl oz (1¼ cups)	warm water (body temperature is best)
15ml	2 tbsp	vegetable oil
60g	2 oz (½ cup)	butter
60g	2 oz (½ cup)	walnuts or almonds
75g	2½ oz (½ cup)	raisins
100g	3½ oz (½ cup)	brown sugar (muscovado)
15g	2 tsp	cinnamon

1. In a large bowl, dissolve yeast in warm water with sugar or honey. Let the liquid rest in a warm place for 10 minutes, until it is bubbly and smells yeasty.

2. Mix in salt and slowly add the flour until the dough comes together into a blob. It should still be soft and slightly sticky to the touch.

3. Sprinkle some flour onto a clean work surface and knead for 10 minutes.

4. Grease a large bowl with vegetable oil. Place the dough in the bowl and cover

5. with a damp tea towel or plastic wrap. Let it rise until double in volume, about 1½ to 2 hours.

6. Press down the dough. Then with a rolling pin, roll it into a flat rectangle 50cm by 25cm (20 in by 10 in). Use extra flour to make sure it does not stick to the counter.

7. Spread melted butter on the dough. Then evenly sprinkle with sugar, nuts, raisins and cinnamon. Roll into a long log.

8. Cut log into 2½cm (1 in) discs and place these flat on a greased sheet. Leave 1cm (½ in) space between rolls for rising, so that they grow into their neighbours. Let them rise for ½ hour.

9. Bake in a preheated oven at 190°C /375°F/ Gas Mark 5 for 20 minutes.

10. Cool slightly on wire rack. Serve when they are still warm and they will melt in your mouth.

Sesame breadsticks

A fun nutritious snack that gives good practice for cutting straight lines. Breadsticks are delicious served with soups and salads or on their own.

Ingredients for 32 long bread sticks

Metric	Imperial/US	
285g	10 oz (2¼ cups)	whole wheat bread flour
285g	10 oz (2¼ cups)	strong bread flour
15g	1 tbsp	natural sugar
10g	1 tsp	sea salt
10g	1 tbsp	dried yeast (not 'quick acting')
300ml	10 fl oz (1¼ cups)	warm water (body temperature is best)
30ml	2 tbsp	olive oil
50g	1¾ oz (¼ cup)	sesame seeeds

1. In a large bread bowl, dissolve yeast and sugar in warm water. Let the liquid rest in a warm place for 10 minutes, until it is bubbly and smells yeasty.

2. Mix in oil, flour and salt and knead for 10 minutes. This is my favourite time to knead a blessing and thankfulness right into the dough.

3. Once the dough is elastic and well mixed, place in oiled bowl and let rise for 1 to 1½ hours or until the dough has doubled in volume. Cover with plastic or a damp cloth to prevent drying.

4. Roll the dough into a rectangle 40cm by 15cm (16 in by 6 in) with a rolling pin. A little oil on the work surface will keep the dough from sticking.

5. Lightly brush the top of the dough with water. Sprinkle sesame seeds onto dough and gently press them into the top of the dough.

6. With a sharp knife cut the dough into strips 12mm (½in) wide. Place on greased baking sheets allowing 12mm (½in) space for expansion.

7. Bake them for 15 minutes in a preheated oven at 220°C /425°F/Gas Mark 7 or until golden and crisp.

8. Cool and serve.

'Children come back to my kindergarten and still comment on the wonderful smell of fresh baked bread. This has stayed with them all these years.'

A retired kindergarten teacher

Cheesy snails

These rolled buns are colourful and fun to make. They have all the flavours of pizza but rolled up into little snails, they excite the taste buds as well as the imagination.

Ingredients for 20 cheesy snails

Metric	Imperial/US	
250g	8 oz (2 cups)	strong white flour (hard or bread flour)
250g	8oz (2 cups)	plain white flour
12g	1 tbsp	raw sugar or honey
24g	2 tsp	sea salt
5g	2 tsp	dried yeast (not 'quick acting')
120ml	4 fl oz (½ cup)	warm water (body temperature is best)
45ml	3 tbsp	olive oil
300ml	10 fl oz (1¼ cups)	herbed tomato sauce (pasta sauce is fine)
15ml	1 tbsp	olive oil
175g	6 oz (1½ cups)	grated cheddar cheese

1. In a large bowl dissolve yeast in warm water with sugar/honey. Let the liquid rest in a warm place for 10 minutes, until it is bubbly and smells yeasty.

2. Stir in the tomato sauce, olive oil, and salt. Slowly add the flour until the dough comes together into a blob. It should still be soft and slightly sticky to the touch.

3. Sprinkle some flour onto a clean work surface and knead for 10 minutes.

4. Grease a large bowl with vegetable oil. Place the dough in the bowl and cover with a damp tea towel or plastic wrap. Let it rise until double in volume, about 1½ to 2 hours.

5. Press down dough. Punching down the dough gives the wrong impression to children. It is much better to treat it gently and to press the air from it. Then with a rolling pin roll it into a flat rectangle 50 by 25cm (20 by 10 inches).

6. Place grated cheese onto the dough and roll into a long log.

7. Cut log into 2½cm (1 in) discs and place these standing on edge on a greased sheet. Let rise for ½ hour. Here you can give shape to the snails' heads by pinching out 2 antennae.

8. Bake in preheated oven at 200°C /400°F/ Gas Mark 6 for 20 minutes.

'One thing I always did with the children was to feel the warm water before adding the "yeast fairies", making sure it was neither too hot nor too cold. We would then cover the yeast fairies so that they could wake up slowly. Sometimes we peeked on them and could see them waking up! We tried not to make any loud noises lest we should scare them away from building their homes in the bread. Ultimately, those kind and generous yeast fairies offered their bubbly homes for our meal. Our imaginations had come alive in the bread.'

Kindergarten teacher

Campfire bread

It is so exciting to cook outdoors over a fire. This recipe allows you to prepare the dough ahead of time then to bake it over an open campfire, wherever you may be. Campfire bread takes a bit more skill and patience than, say, marshmallows, but it is delicious on its own or with a meal.

Ingredients for 12 servings

Metric	Imperial/US	
400g	14 oz (3½ cups)	plain flour
25g	2 tbsp	natural sugar
18g	1 tbsp	sea salt
12g	1 tbsp	baking powder
60g	2 oz (¼ cups)	softened butter
170ml	6 fl oz (¾ cup)	warm water

In the kitchen

1. Mix together all dry ingredients in a large bowl.

2. Add water and stir. Dough should be too dry to come together into one lump.

3. Cut in butter and knead by hand just long enough to make it smooth and consistent.

4. Form into a log, wrap in plastic and keep in the refrigerator for up to 3 days.

At the campsite

5. Prepare 1 or more sticks 2cm (1 in) in diameter by shaving clean with a pocket knife.

6. Cut dough into 12 pieces. Roll into long, pencil thin snakes 30cm (12 in) and coil these around the end of a stick.

7. Hold the sticks high over the fire or coals, turning continuously until the coiled dough is baked golden brown.

8. Cool and eat right off the stick.

As I was baking campfire bread the other night over an open fire at Emerson College, an older woman became very interested in what I was doing. She must have been in her seventies and asked if she could have a try. I wrapped a coil of dough on a stick for her and she baked it over the fire. She was an expert. She said this was just how she had made bread as a young girl growing up in South Africa. And the taste of it brought forth a flood of memories, which she delighted in sharing with us.

FESTIVE BREADS

Dragon bread

Dragons are important symbols in both east and west. While bringing good fortune for the Chinese New Year, they are more an ill omen in western culture. Dragons bring great challenges and fears to be conquered especially around the Michaelmas season, 29th September. Does your dragon bring good fortune or is it one that needs taming? Dragon bread is a wonderful way to explore with children the different moods of Michaelmas or the Chinese New Year. Making and presenting a dragon loaf can call forth a creative and courageous spirit. In autumn, for Michaelmas, bake a dragon and then decorate it with colourful leaves, flowers and fruits of the harvest. In midwinter, for the Chinese New Year, use nuts and dried fruits to decorate this symbol of good fortune.

Ingredients for 1 large dragon

METRIC	IMPERIAL/US	
375g	12oz (3 cups)	strong wholemeal flour
375g	12oz (3 cups)	strong bread flour
240g	8 fl oz (1 cup)	pumpkin or sweet potato (cooked or canned)
60g	2 oz (¼ cup)	raw sugar or honey
24g	2 tsp	sea salt
7g	1 flat tbsp	dried yeast (not 'quick acting')
240ml	8 fl oz (1 cup)	warm water (body temperature is best)
30ml	2 tbsp	vegetable oil
		2 eggs
10g	1 tbsp	ground cinnamon
3g	1 tsp	ground nutmeg
125g	4 oz (½ cup)	dried fruits and nuts to decorate (optional)

1. In a large bowl, dissolve yeast in warm water with sugar/ honey. Let the liquid rest in a warm place for 10 minutes, until it is frothy and smells yeasty. If the water is too hot (above 50°C or 120°F) this will kill the yeast. If it is too cold everything will proceed very slowly.

2. Mix in pumpkin, eggs, oil, salt and spices. Then slowly add the flour until it all comes together. The dough should still be soft and slightly sticky to the touch.

3. Sprinkle flour onto a clean work surface and knead the dough, folding in loose flour so that the dough is elastic but does not stick to your hands or the counter. Knead with vigour for 10 minutes. This is the perfect time to sing a bread song or to knead a blessing right into the dough.

4. Grease a large bowl with vegetable oil. Place the dough in the bowl and cover with a moist tea towel or with plastic wrap to keep in moisture. Let the dough rise in a warm place for 1½ to 2 hours until it doubles in volume.

5. Press down the dough. Punching down the dough gives the wrong impression to children. It is much better to treat it gently and press the air from it. Then shape into a dragon. This can be done either in one large loaf or with smaller loaves that can then be joined together. Make sure to exaggerate any shapes, as the rising dough will tend to lose its definition. Keep in mind that thinner parts will cook more quickly in the oven.

6. Bake in a preheated oven at 190°C /375°F/ Gas Mark 5 for 30 to 40 minutes or until golden brown. The underside will give a hollow, wooden sound when tapped with a finger.

7. Let the dragon cool and decorate as a centrepiece.

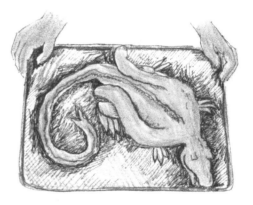

'Every year at Michaelmas time the children in my school looked forward to making, then devouring, dragons based on this recipe. Our dragons usually turned out looking rather sweet with puffy wings, round bellies and almond eyes, hardly the creatures of nightmares. They all had such personality, revealing something special about their creators. Sometimes they were so cute it was hard to eat them and I had to slice them up beyond view of the children.'

Creative options

- stuff the dragon's belly with dried fruits and nuts, the dragon's hidden jewels
- paint with egg white for a shiny crust
- decorate with almonds

Harvest spelt bread

As an older cousin of wheat, spelt is more easily tolerated by some people who are wheat-sensitive. It is a soft grain with very little gluten, but lots of flavour, well worth a try. This harvest spelt recipe can also be made with 100 percent spelt flour. Loaves will be dense and rich.

Ingredients for 1 harvest loaf

Metric	Imperial/US	
250g	8 oz (2 cups)	spelt flour
250g	8oz (2 cups)	strong white bread flour
30ml	2 tbsp	honey
24g	2 tsp	sea salt
5g	2 tsp	dried yeast (not 'quick acting')
300ml	10 fl oz (1¼ cups)	warm water (body temperature is best)
10g	1 tbsp	orange zest

1. In a large bowl dissolve yeast in warm water with honey. Let the liquid rest in a warm place for 10 minutes, until it is frothy and smells yeasty.

2. Mix in salt and zest and slowly add the flour until the dough comes together into a blob. It should still be soft and slightly sticky to the touch.

3. Sprinkle some flour onto a clean work surface and knead for 10 minutes. This is my favourite time to knead a blessing and thankfulness right into the dough.

4. Place dough in a large greased bowl and cover with plastic or a damp tea towel. Let it rise 1 to 1½ hours until double in volume. Keep a careful eye on it because spelt generally rises more quickly than wheat dough.

5. Press down dough. Give small mouse-sized pieces to each child and divide the remainder

into 3 even balls. Roll these long and thin. Then plait (braid) them together. Have the children make little animals to place on top of the plait. Let rise for ½ hour or until volume has doubled.

6.   Bake in a preheated oven at 190°C /375°F/ Gas Mark 5 for 30 minutes or until golden brown. Let cool before eating.

'We make bread in my kindergarten every week, using a mixture of spelt, rye and barley flour. Children come to help by choice. With aprons and washed hands, they help mix the dough, pour the water and add the flour. My assistant kneads the dough, giving the children little bits to make decorations for the top of the loaves. They make mice and birds, among other things. Sometimes she gives older children (with bigger hands) a piece of dough to knead the main part of the loaves. Children also enjoy scrubbing the dough off the table and watching the loaves go in and come out the oven.'

Challah

Challah is a traditional Jewish bread prepared each Friday to celebrate the Sabbath, the day of rest. The dough is made with eggs, and sweetened with honey. Braided from three or four strands, it is then brushed with egg to give it a golden colour. Poppy or sesame seeds can be sprinkled on top before baking. The seeds represent the manna God gave the Israelites to eat when they were wandering for 40 years in the desert.

Ingredients for 2 braided loaves

METRIC	IMPERIAL/US	
250g	8 oz (2 cups)	plain flour
300ml	10 fl oz (1¼ cups)	warm water
25g	2 tbsp	natural sugar or honey
24g	2 tsp	sea salt
80g	3 oz (⅓ cup)	softened butter
10g	1 tbsp	dried yeast (not 'quick acting')
		3 beaten eggs (save a little for the glaze.
		Add an equal amount of water to brush on the
		top of the loaves)
20g	2 tsp	poppy or sesame seeds

1. In a large bowl, dissolve yeast in warm water with sugar/ honey. Let the liquid rest in a warm place for 10 minutes, until it is frothy and smells yeasty.

2. Mix in eggs, butter, salt and slowly add the flour until the dough comes together. It should still be soft and slightly sticky to the touch.

3. Sprinkle some flour onto a clean work surface and knead for 10 minutes. Challah is a bread of celebration and gratitude. You can knead a blessing and your thankfulness right into the dough. The Hebrew prayer (page 150) is perfect here.

4. Grease a large bowl with vegetable oil. Place the dough in the bowl and cover with a damp tea towel. Let it rise until double in volume, about 1½ to 2 hours.

'I did not know how bread was made until I was an adult. I thought it just came in packets.'

5. Press down dough and divide in half. Then cut each half into 4 even balls. Roll these long and thin and join them at one end. Then plait (braid) them together – see below.

6. Brush the tops with beaten egg and water and sprinkle with seeds. Bake in a preheated oven at 190°C /375°F/Gas Mark 5 for 40 minutes or until golden brown.

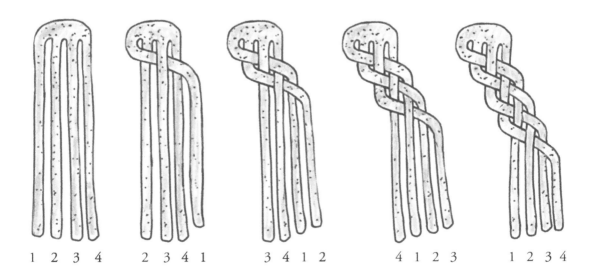

1 2 3 4   2 3 4 1   3 4 1 2   4 1 2 3   1 2 3 4

Santa Lucia buns

The feast day of Santa Lucia is celebrated throughout Sweden as a festival of lights. On 13th December, in the early hours of the morning, a young woman dresses in a white gown with a red sash and a crown with blazing candles. She goes from house to house delivering fresh baked saffron buns and warm milk to all the children. Every village has its own Lucia and these are the buns she carries in her basket.

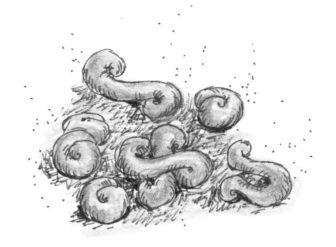

Ingredients for 12 buns

Metric	Imperial/US	
500g	1 lb (4 cups)	plain flour
5g	2 tsp	dried yeast (not 'quick acting')
100g	3½ oz (½ cup)	natural sugar
1g	1 tsp	saffron powder
180ml	6 fl oz (¾ cup)	warm milk
60g	2 oz (¼ cup)	softened butter
24g	2 tsp	sea salt
31g	1 oz (¼ cup)	raisins or currants
1.5g	½ tsp	ground cardamom
		2 eggs. I for the dough, 1 for egg glaze
15g	2 tbsp	chopped almonds for topping
12g	1 tbsp	coarsely crushed demerara sugar for topping

1. Dissolve sugar, yeast and saffron powder in warm milk. Leave in warm place for 10 minutes until frothy.

2. Beat 1 egg. Add this to yeast.

3. Stir in salt, cardamom and flour.

4. Cut in butter and add raisins.

5. Knead thoroughly, return to greased bowl, cover and allow to rise for 1½ hours or until doubled.

6. Preheat oven to 200°C /400°F/Gas Mark 6.

7. Divide dough into 12 pieces. Roll into 20cm (8 in) long snakes. Coil snakes starting from both ends and meeting in the middle, making a spiraled 'S'.

8. Put on greased baking tray. Brush with beaten egg, sprinkle with coarse sugar and almonds. Let rise for ½ hour or until doubled.

9. Bake for 10-12 minutes until golden brown.

10. Cool and serve with warm milk or coffee.

Hot cross buns

Hot cross buns are often made for Good Friday before Easter. There is much debate about the origin of the cross glazed on each bun. Some say it dates back to the 12th century, when a monk placed it there to honour Good Friday, the Day of the Cross. Supposedly, this pastry was the only thing permitted to enter the mouths of the faithful on this holy day. Other accounts talk of an English widow, whose son went off to sea. She vowed to bake him a bun every Good Friday. When he didn't return she continued to bake a hot cross bun for him each year and hang it in the bakery window in good faith he would return some day.

Ingredients for 12 buns

METRIC	IMPERIAL/US	
400g	14 oz (3 ½ cups)	plain flour
250ml	8 fl oz (1 cup)	warm milk
25g	2 tbsp	natural sugar
30g	2 tbsp	softened butter
5g	½ tsp	sea salt
5g	2 tsp	dried yeast (not 'quick acting')
		1 egg
1.5g	½ tsp	cinnamon
1.5g	½ tsp	nutmeg
31g	1 oz (¼ cup)	currants
20g	2 tbsp	candied orange peel

FOR GLAZE

		1 egg yolk
15ml	1 tbsp	water

ICING FOR CROSS

50g	2 oz (¼ cup)	confectioners' (icing) sugar
2.5ml	½ tsp	vanilla extract
7.5ml	1½ tsp	milk

1. Dissolve sugar and yeast in warm milk. Leave for 15 minutes until frothy.

2. Add salt, spices, egg, peel, currants and butter.

3. Add flour and knead thoroughly. Return to oiled bowl, cover and allow to rise for 1½hours or until doubled.

4. Press down the dough. Then shape into 12 small buns. Put these on a greased tray and let rise for ½ hour or until doubled.

5. Brush each bun with egg yoke glaze for a shiny brown crust.

6. Bake at 200°C/400°F/Gas Mark 6 for 12 minutes until golden brown.

7. In a small dish, stir confectioners' sugar with vanilla. Add milk slowly, just enough to make the icing flow.

8. Cool buns and paint a cross with icing by letting it drizzle from a spoon.

9. Serve warm with milk or coffee.

'This is how it was meant to be! Fresh baked bread seemed so natural as a child and still brings back wonderful memories of childhood.'

Easter bread

This light sweet bread can be made as a braided ring to hold Easter chicks, eggs and candy, or sweets. It can also be formed into individual bread chicks that hold coloured eggs. These can be both decorative, and delicious, centrepieces for your festival table.

Ingredients for 2 Easter loaves or 8 chicks

METRIC	IMPERIAL/US	
750g	1 lb 8oz (6 cups)	plain flour
20g	2 tbsp	dried yeast (not 'quick acting')
		4 eggs
250g	9 oz (1 cup)	natural sugar
125ml	4 fl oz (½ cup)	orange juice
20g	4 tsp	candied orange peel
180ml	6 fl oz (¾ cup)	melted butter
15g	1 tbsp	ground cardamom seeds
125ml	4 fl oz (½ cup)	milk
2.5g	½ tsp	saffron

FOR GLAZE		
40g	2 tbsp	confectioners' (icing) sugar
5ml	1 tsp	Almond essence (extract)

1. In a large bowl, dissolve saffron in warm milk. Add sugar and yeast. Stir and leave to rise for 10 minutes.

2. Stir in beaten eggs, butter, orange juice, orange peel and cardamom.

3. Add flour and lightly knead until all the ingredients come together. It should still be soft and slightly sticky to the touch. Add more flour as needed.

4. Let it rise for 1½ hours or until doubled.

5. Press down and divide the dough in six equal pieces. Roll each long and thin then plait (braid) into two loaves. Tuck ends of plait under loaves and place on greased baking sheet.

6. Let rise for ½ hour.

7. Bake in preheated oven at 180°C /350°F/ Gas Mark 4 for 40 minutes.

8. Mix almond extract and sugar together. Brush this on the Easter bread after it comes out of the oven while it is still hot.

I sometimes place whole uncooked eggs on the braided dough, which rises up and bakes around the eggs, baking the eggs too. An alternative is to place egg-shaped stones and bake. Replace these later with dyed Easter eggs.

To make Easter chicks that hold dyed or cooked eggs:

1. Divide the risen dough into 8 even pieces.

2. Take two-thirds of each piece and make an oblong body. Place on a greased baking tray. Allow 2cm (1 in) for expansion.

3. Place an egg or an egg-sized stone into the middle of the body.

4. Make a ball with the other third. This will be the head.

5. Join the two together and pinch a beak and a tail.

6. Just before you put these in the oven, pinch these out again.

7. Bake for only 25 minutes.

8. Glaze if desired, as for the loaves.

QUICK BREADS

These old favourites can be baked from start to finish in less than an hour. They are real crowd pleasers. Instead of yeast, they rely on the chemical activity of baking powder and / or bicarbonate of soda (baking soda) to help the dough to rise. Most quick breads do not require kneading and thus make less of a mess in the kitchen.

While walking on the West Highland Way in Scotland, I met a woman who shared this memory from her childhood. 'As a child the best part of baking was where my mum and I used to mix the batter and sugar together with our bare hands. Making cakes was such fun! I only wish she would have taught me how to bake bread too.'

Devon scones

Homemade scones are a simple treat for teatime. I like them best served hot with butter and jam. They are also delicious with honey or cheese.

Ingredients for 8 scones

Metric	Imperial/US	
170g	6 oz (1½ cups)	plain (soft or pastry) flour
5g	2 tsp	baking powder
5g	½ tsp	sea salt
150ml	5 fl oz (½ cup)	milk
60g	2 oz (¼ cup)	butter

1. Sift together flour, salt and baking powder.

2. Cut in softened butter with two knives or a pastry blender.

3. Stir in milk until it is thoroughly mixed.

4. Knead lightly with hands to form it into a ball.

5. Place on a floured surface and flatten dough to 2 cm (¾ in) thickness.

6. Using a glass, cut out circles and place them on a greased tray.

7. Bake for 10 to 12 minutes in a preheated oven at 220°C /425°F/Gas Mark 7.

Variations
- Add 40g /1½ oz poppy seeds
- Add 100g /4 oz cheddar cheese and chives
- Add a handful of currants
- Glaze tops with egg yolk for a shiny surface

Corn bread

Traditional American corn bread baked to a crispy golden brown in an iron skillet is hard to beat. This recipe has real corn kernels mixed in for moister and more flavourful bread. It takes less than an hour to make and tastes great with chilli, stews or just butter.

Ingredients for 1 corn bread, serves 8

Metric	Imperial/US	
		2 ears of fresh corn *or*
250g	8 oz (1 cup)	frozen or canned corn
150g	5 oz (1 cup)	polenta (corn meal)
125g	4 oz (1 cup)	strong bread flour
50g	2 oz (¼ cup)	natural sugar or honey
15g	1 tbsp	baking powder
5g	½ tsp	salt
250ml	8 fl oz (1 cup)	milk or buttermilk
60g	2 fl oz (¼ cup)	melted butter
		2 eggs

1. In a large bowl, mix together all the dry ingredients except the whole corn.

2. Melt butter in 23cm (9 in) cast iron frying pan (or in similar sized cake pan).

3. In another bowl, beat eggs. Then add the milk and melted butter.

4. Stir wet and dry together until smooth. Do not over-stir or the bread will be heavy.

5. Add sweetcorn kernels.

6. Pour into greased frying pan.

7. Bake for 20 minutes in a preheated oven at 190°C /375°F/Gas Mark 5 until golden brown.

8. Cool slightly and cut into wedges to serve.

When I was growing up, we had a rule that helped us as children to share food fairly. My mother always said, 'Whoever cuts the pieces, chooses last.'

Irish soda bread

It was common to make bread using baking soda instead of yeast in parts of rural Ireland. This practice began out of necessity. Baker's yeast works best with strong bread flour, which was scarce in many parts of Ireland. Baking soda, however, could be counted on to leaven bread even with poor flour. When baking soda combines with an acid, such as yoghurt in this recipe, it releases carbon dioxide that instantly causes the bread to rise. This is both a historic and hearty recipe that will stave off even the most savage winter gale.

Ingredients for 1 loaf, serves 8

METRIC	IMPERIAL/US	
250g	8 oz (2 cups)	wholemeal flour
250g	8 oz (2 cups)	plain flour
5g	½ tsp	salt
10g	2 tsp	bicarbonate of soda (baking soda)
60g	2 oz (¼ cup)	butter
250ml	8 fl oz (1 cup)	yogurt or buttermilk
125ml	4 fl oz (½ cup)	milk

1. Preheat oven to 180°C/350°F/Gas Mark 4.

2. In a large bowl mix together all the dry ingredients.

3. Cut in butter with two knives until the chunks are pea-sized.

4. Add milk and yoghurt. Mix to a soft dough.

5. Knead on a lightly floured surface for 1 minute.

6. Shape into a ball and press into 20cm (8 in) disc onto a large greased baking tray. Cut a cross about 2cm (1 in) deep onto the top of the loaf and bake immediately for 45 minutes.

7. Cool on a wire rack and eat while still fresh.

Variations

- For Saint Patrick's Day make Irish soda bread in the form of a four-leafed clover. Divide the dough into 4 equal parts with a little bit left for the stem. Mould into a four-leafed clover on a greased baking sheet. Bake as usual, careful that the thinner stem does not overcook and burn.

- For a sweeter bread, add ½ cup of natural sugar and/or a handful of sultanas or currants.

During the industrial revolution when thousands of families moved from rural communities into overcrowded cities, the quality of bread plummeted. All sorts of things were added to the flour sold to poor people. The Victorian author, Tennyson, wrote:

'For chalk and alum and plaster are sold to the poor for bread. And the spirit of murder works in the very means of life.'
Alfred Tennyson, from Maud

Cranberry nut muffins

Packed with pecans and cranberries, these all-spelt muffins are a treat for the whole family. They are perfect for a weekend breakfast or a quick snack.

See the Muffin Man song on page 135.

Ingredients for 8 muffins

Metric	Imperial/US	
250g	8 oz (2 cups)	spelt flour
12g	1 tbsp	baking powder
3g	¼ tsp	sea salt
120g	4 oz (½ cup)	natural sugar
120g	4 fl oz (½ cup)	sunflower oil
120ml	4 fl oz (½ cup)	yogurt
		2 beaten eggs
150g	5 oz (1½ cups)	sweetened dried cranberries
100g	3½ oz (1 cup)	chopped walnuts

1. Mix flour, salt, sugar and baking powder in a large bowl.

2. In a separate bowl, mix together wet ingredients: oil, yoghurt and egg.

3. Stir together as little as is needed. Too much stirring makes the muffins stiff!

4. Fold in the dried cranberries and walnuts.

5. Spoon into greased muffin tins level with top. If any tins are left empty, fill them with 1cm of water to ensure even baking.

6. Bake for 20 minutes in a preheated oven at 180°C /350°F/Gas Mark 4.

7. Eat while still warm.

'When all is well prepared behind the scenes, then it all goes well. And if not, at least you can recover from the minor catastrophes.'

An experienced baker

Gingerbread men

Gingerbread men are fun to make at any time of the year. They are delicious plain or decorated with coloured sugar icings. This recipe can also be used to build the walls and roof of a gingerbread house. The story of the Gingerbread Man is on page 20.

Ingredients for fourteen 14cm (5 in) gingerbread men

Metric	Imperial/US	
100g	3½ oz (½ cup)	softened butter
100g	3½ oz (½ cup)	brown sugar (muscovado)
150g	6 fl oz (¾ cup)	molasses
		1 egg
360g	13 oz (3 cups)	sifted plain (soft or pastry) flour
2g	¼ tsp	sea salt
5g	1 tsp	bicarbonate of soda (baking soda)
5g	1 tsp	baking powder
4g	1 tsp	ground ginger
2g	½ tsp	cinammon
2g	½ tsp	ground cloves

1. In a large bowl, cream together butter and sugar until smooth. Stir in molasses and egg.

2. In another bowl combine flour, salt, baking powder, baking soda, ginger, cinnamon and cloves.

3. Blend dry ingredients into the wet mixture until smooth. Cover, and chill for at least 30 minutes.

4. On a lightly floured surface, roll the dough out to ½ cm (¼ in) thickness.

5. Cut into men or other shapes with cookie cutters or knives. Place cookies 1cm (½ in) apart on greased baking sheets.

6. Preheat the oven to 180°C /350°F/Gas Mark 4. Bake for 8 to 10 minutes or until firm.

7. Let cool on wire racks before eating or decorate with coloured icing.

Almond rice muffins

Almonds and rice flour make light and crunchy muffins with an essence of marzipan. These go well with green tea.

Ingredients for 8 muffins

Metric	Imperial/US	
120g	4 oz (1 cup)	brown rice flour
120g	4 oz (1 cup)	plain white flour
15g	1 tbsp	baking powder
120g	4 oz (½ cup)	natural sugar
3g	¼ tsp	sea salt
120ml	4 fl oz (½ cup)	sunflower oil
120ml	4 fl oz (½ cup)	yogurt
		2 beaten eggs
150g	1 tbsp (1½ cups)	chopped almonds

1. Mix flour, salt, sugar and baking powder in a large bowl.

2. In a separate bowl, mix together wet ingredients: oil, yoghurt and egg.

3. Stir together. Too much stirring makes muffins stiff!

4. Fold coarsely chopped almonds into the batter.

5. Spoon batter into greased muffin tins level with top. If any tins are left empty fill them half full with water to ensure even baking.

6. Decorate tops of muffins with whole almonds.

7. Bake for 20 minutes in a preheated oven at 180°C / 350°F/Gas Mark 4.

8. Eat while still warm.

SOURDOUGH BREADS

Making a sourdough culture

I bake most of my bread with a sourdough leaven rather than commercial (fresh or dried) yeast. I have been using the same starter for years now and have shared it with family and friends around the world. I enjoy its taste and find it both more flexible to work with and easier to digest.

A sourdough starter makes the most flavourful breads and certainly the most nutritious, because it has begun the digestive process for you. It breaks down complex carbohydrates and other nutrients into more digestible forms so that the body can more readily assimilate the vitamins, minerals and other nutrition. This breaking-down of components also makes sourdough easier for people with wheat sensitivities or allergies to digest it. The process releases more of the grain's flavour and naturally prevents spoilage. And, last but not least, it is free. You can make your own and keep it for years.

It's also a fascinating way for children to learn about biology. A sourdough starter, culture or natural leaven is a living community of yeasts and bacteria growing in a controlled mixture of flour and water. There can be hundreds of different organisms involved.

Making a sourdough culture, or natural leaven, is a process as old as bread-baking itself. It's not something we see much of these days. Perhaps we are less used to making things that take time to mature. Besides, we are rather hypersensitive to germs and cleanliness, and perhaps a little uneasy at allowing yeast and bacteria to multiply and go sour in our kitchens. Nevertheless, making a sourdough starter can be a simple, straight-forward and hygienically safe process.

Sourdough can be started in any kitchen. Each will have its unique quality and flavour. Some cultures make sour and tangy breads like San Francisco sourdough, while others can be quite sweet and nutty, as I prefer. It all depends on the many variables in temperature, humidity, quality of water and flour, what else is cooked in the kitchen as well as the mood of the cooks in the kitchen.

Making your own sourdough culture

There are plenty of more complicated ways, but this straightforward one works time and again, and is quite resilient to mistakes. You can approach making a starter as a bit of a science experiment. Older children will enjoy charting its progress and observing with all their senses the changes that happen each day. All you need is organic, strong (bread or hard) flour and purified or spring water. If using tap water, let it sit in an open vessel for a day so that the chlorine evaporates.

Day 1

Mix equal amounts of pure, room temperature water (not chlorinated) and flour in a bowl. Use 15ml (1 tbsp) of each. Stir together and let sit uncovered in a cool part of your kitchen. If there are flies or other insects then cover the mixture with plastic wrap or cheesecloth. Everything that is needed for the sourdough starter is already in the wheat and water.

Day 2

Add another 15ml (1 tbsp) of both water and flour. Stir and let sit in a cool place.

Day 3

Add 30ml (2 tbsp) of both water and flour, stir and let sit. Has the smell changed, perhaps a little?

Day 4

Add 60ml (4 tbsp) of both water and flour, stir and let sit. Each day you are in effect doubling the volume of the mixture. By now you should notice some bubbling and a sour, possibly unpleasant, smell.

Day 5

At this point it is easiest to reduce the volume of the culture. You only need a tiny bit, 15ml (1 tbsp), to continue developing the flavour and vitality of the culture. You can either compost most of it or better yet, add it to enhance the taste of another bread recipe. Bakers call adding a bit of older dough to a recipe a 'poolish'. It adds some of the sourdough flavour and elasticity to any yeasted dough.

Day 6 to Day 14

Continue doubling the volume each day. The culture should be bubbly and elastic. The sour smell should become more sweet and nutty by now and, if so, it is ready to use.

- If at any time the culture smells too sour or alcoholic, or begins to look lifeless then add more flour and move it to a cooler place. It may be that the culture is developing more rapidly in your kitchen because it is warm.
- Instead of doubling once a day, try every 12 hours.
- Even if you think you have made a complete disaster, compost all but 15ml (1 tbsp) and continue to double.

Now you are ready to bake, using your culture in one of the following recipes.

Make sure to save a ball of today's dough as your starter for the next time you bake. If you only bake once a week, or every few weeks, then it is best to store your starter kneaded stiff with lots of flour in a jar in the refrigerator. The starter will grow, so make sure that the lid is loose-fitting. This will keep for up to four weeks without needing any attention. If you are worried you can always feed the starter by doubling it with water and more flour. Then put it back in the refrigerator. If ever it gets mouldy, scrape the mouldy portion off and double the rest. It may be slow to start but will most likely bounce right back.

You can even store your starter in the freezer if you will not be using it for more than a month. Knead in flour until it is stiff and then doubly wrap it in cling film so that it is airtight but able to expand. When you are preparing to bake again, take it from the freezer a day early and double it with water and fresh flour. Slowly it will come back to life ready to leaven your next loaves.

Once you get used to working with sourdough you might never want to go back to commercial yeast. It takes some patience, but little more work than yeasted dough. In fact it can be much more flexible, allowing you to work when it suits your schedule. Simply go as far as you can with a recipe and then cover the dough and put it in the refrigerator until you can carry on with the next steps. It is remarkably forgiving and flexible.

Some bakers use a different leavening culture for wheat and rye breads. I have found, by accident, that for the home baker the same culture can work equally well for both types of bread, and spelt too. So now I just have one natural leaven starter for all my baking needs. If you are baking for wheat-sensitive

people, then it is better to have a truly wheat-free starter made entirely from rye flour. This can be developed in the same way and works beautifully.

In some of my workshops, participants can get pretty carried away with their enthusiasm for bread experiments. I rarely discourage this. One gentleman became so enamoured with the process of baking with sourdough leaven that he began composing haiku. He captured the essence of sourdough in only 14 syllables! In sharing his bread and poetry (he wrote a series of sourdough haiku) he inspired others to write creatively about their passions and discoveries with bread. In the end they compiled a small magazine entitled *Twenty ways to look at bread.*

Sourdough starter haiku

Natural yeasts
Awaiting cultivation
Flour, water, patience.

Michael Moran

To me, bread is life
The symbol of Christ's body
Broken for sharing

Fran

Country hearth loaves

This is the way bread is meant to taste with a crispy crust, airy crumb and plenty of tangy flavour. The taste of these sourdough loaves will transport you to the way bread used to taste in much of Europe.

Ingredients for 2 loaves

Metric	Imperial/US	
600g	1 lb 4 oz (5 cups)	strong bread flour
250g	8 oz (2 cups)	coarse wholemeal or rye flour
500ml	16 fl oz (2 cups)	water (room temperature)
250ml	8 fl oz (1 cup)	sourdough starter
18g	1 tbsp	sea salt

1. In the evening, mix sourdough starter with 500ml water and 400g of the flour. Stir vigorously and let sit overnight in a cool place.

2. The next morning (8 to 12 hours later), the starter should be bubbly, tangy-smelling and ready to go. Stir in the rest of the flour.

3. Remove 250ml /8 fl oz (1 cup) of this dough to use as starter for your next baking. Put this in a glass or ceramic jar in the refrigerator, where it should last for 2 weeks or more. Knead in more flour if you want it to last longer.

4. Add salt. Stir in as much of the rest of the flour as it takes to make the dough firm. When it becomes too difficult to stir, place the dough on a floured surface and knead with energy for a good 10 minutes until the dough is uniform and elastic with strong gluten fibres. This will help it rise and be light and airy. Add only enough flour so the dough does not stick to the counter or your hands.

5. Let the dough rest for 15 minutes. Here is the perfect interval to tell a story or sing a song.

6. Divide into 2 loaves and shape into rounds by stretching and folding the dough. Surface tension helps the loaves rise up rather than

spread. Seal the seams on the underside of the loaves. Coat the entire loaf with flour, especially on the underside to prevent sticking. This flour helps to a form a good skin and helps the loaves to rise upwards. Place loaves on a floured baking sheet and let rise in a warm place for 2 to 3 hours until doubled.

7. Preheat oven to 180°C /350°F/Gas Mark 4. Slit the tops of the loaves with a sharp knife to allow for expansion. Bake for 40 minutes or until golden brown and the undersides give a hollow, wooden sound when tapped with a finger.

8. Cool on a wire rack before slicing to complete the baking process.

Variations

*   Add a little of all the 7 grains (see page 178) in the recipe at step 1.

*   Substitute up to 250g / 8 oz (2 cups) rolled grains, grain flour, sprouted and /or cooked grains.

*   If moist grains are added, then more flour may be kneaded in to attain the same elastic and smooth consistency.

One woman, now a grandmother, can still remember the reverential way her mother would cut two slits crosswise into the top of each loaf before she put it in the oven. 'Nothing needed to be said. This was a religious experience pure and simple.'

Sunny wheat sourdough

Orange zest, honey and sunflower seeds give this
whole wheat bread a sweet and nutty flavour.

Ingredients for 2 loaves

Metric	Imperial/US	
800g	1 lb 8 oz (6½ cups)	whole wheat bread flour
500ml	16 fl oz (2 cups)	water (room temperature)
250ml	8 fl oz (1 cup)	sourdough starter
10g	1tsp	sea salt
10g	1 tbsp	orange zest/grated rind of 1 orange
120g	4 oz (1 cup)	sunflower seeds
80ml	3 fl oz (⅓ cup)	honey

1. In the evening, mix sourdough starter with 500ml water and 400g of the flour. Stir vigorously and let sit overnight in a cool place.

2. The next morning (8 to 12 hours later), the starter should be bubbly, tangy-smelling and ready to go. Stir in the rest of the flour.

3. Remove 250ml /8 fl oz (1 cup) of this dough to use as starter for your next baking. Put this in a glass or ceramic jar in the refrigerator, where it should last for 2 weeks or more. Knead in more flour if you want it to last longer.

4. Add honey, orange zest and salt. Stir in as much of the rest of the flour as it takes to make the dough firm. When it becomes too difficult to stir, place the dough on a floured surface and knead with energy for a good 10 minutes until the dough is uniform and elastic with strong gluten fibres. Add only enough flour that the dough does not stick to the counter or your hands.

5. Let the dough rest for 15 minutes. Here is the perfect interval to tell a story or sing a song.

6. Knead in sunflower seeds. Divide into 2 loaves and shape into rounds by stretching and folding the dough to create tension to help the loaves to rise upwards. When the tops are smooth, pinch together the seams on the underside of the loaves. Coat the undersides with flour to prevent sticking. Place loaves on a floured baking sheet and let rise in a warm place for 2 to 3 hours until doubled.

7. Preheat oven to 180°C /350°F/Gas Mark 4. Slit the tops of the loaves with a sharp knife to allow for expansion. Bake for 40 minutes or until golden brown and the undersides give a hollow, wooden sound when tapped with a finger.

8. Cool on a wire rack before slicing to complete the baking process.

'As a child I loved to play in the sandpit a lot, baking imaginary cakes and loaves. I was fascinated watching my mother doing the real thing. She always admonished me for looking into the oven when the bread was baking, saying the loaves would not rise properly. I did not always listen. In this way, I was not always such a good girl.'

Old World rye

Rye has long been the favoured grain of Northern Europe, valued for its hardiness in growing, as well as its distinctive flavour.

This traditional recipe makes moist, rich bread that tastes great and keeps well for several weeks. It is satisfying either on its own or topped with butter and mature cheese. Because it uses only rye flour, no manual kneading is necessary. It can go straight from the mixing bowl into tins without any mess or extra work.

Ingredients for 2 small loaves

Metric	Imperial/US	
500g	1 lb (4 cups)	rye flour
500ml	16 fl oz (2 cups)	water (room temperature)
250ml	8 fl oz (1 cup)	sourdough starter
18g	1 tbsp	sea salt

1. In the evening, mix sourdough starter with all the water and half of the flour. Stir vigorously and let sit overnight in a comfortably cool place.

2. The next morning (or after 4 to 12 hours depending on temperature when the mixture becomes frothy with bubbles) remove 250ml /8 fl oz (about 1 cup) dough to use as starter for your next baking. Add flour to the starter to make it stiffer. Put this in a glass or ceramic jar in the refrigerator, where it should last for up to 4 weeks.

3. Add salt and stir in flour. The dough should be sticky and moist. You can mix it either with a spoon or your hands, but kneading is not essential, as the rye does not have as much of the protein gluten as does wheat and relies on starches and proteins to hold the trapped gases that make it rise.

4. Grease 2 small (1 lb) loaf bread tins. Smaller tins allow the inside of this moist bread to fully cook. Spoon the sticky dough into them. Then use a wet spoon to smooth the tops of the loaves. Allow the loaves to rise for 2 to 3 hours or until they double in volume in a cool place. Warmer temperatures make every step happen more quickly, and also give the bread a sourer flavour. Cooler temperatures slow down the

process and allow a sweeter flavour to mature in the loaves. You will have to experiment to see what works best in your kitchen.

5. Bake the loaves in a preheated oven at 180°C /350°F/Gas Mark 4 for 40 minutes or until done. Let loaves cool before cutting them in thin slices.

Storing

*   If properly stored in a wooden or ceramic vessel where the rye loaves can breathe, they can keep for weeks. The flavour reaches its peak 2 days after baking.
*   If the loaves dry out, moisten by briefly running a loaf under some water. Then warm it in the oven at medium heat for 10 minutes. Or cut and moisten individual slices and toast them.

A woman shared this bread story from her childhood:
'I grew up in a village high in the Swiss Alps. It had a community bake house with a wood oven that we fired up once a month. We did not need to bake more often because sourdough rye keeps fresh for so long. The old men had the job of stoking the oven fire, which they did while sharing the village news. When the fire was hot enough, their job was done. Then each housewife would bring her dough to the bake house to rise and be baked in the oven. When she had finished, she would knock on the door of her neighbour, no matter how late the hour, to let her know it was her turn. It took three days and three nights for the entire village to bake all its bread. This is how rye bread has been baked for as long as anyone can remember and is still going on.'

117

LEFTOVER BREAD

What to do with all those leftover bits of flour and stale ends of loaves? If you have a sourdough starter then you can simply feed it with any leftover bits of flour from your counter or mixing bowl. Nothing is wasted. And with leftover ends of loaves and rolls, it is best to let them go fully dry and stale. Then you can save them to make an old favourite, bread pudding.

Large amounts of bread is not good for birds, but crumbs will do no harm. The robins and the tom-tits come to my window every morning to see what I have left for them. They make wonderful early morning companions as I eat fresh toast at the breakfast table.

Bread and butter pudding

First known as a 'poor man's pudding', bread and butter pudding is an old fashioned dessert popular in England since the 13th century. It is a great way to make use of all your stale ends and leftover rolls. Nuts, zests, candied or fresh fruit can also be added.

Ingredients to serve 6 to 8 people

METRIC	IMPERIAL/US	
250g	8 oz (approx 3 cups)	stale bread
150g	5 oz (1 cup)	currants or raisins
50g	2 oz (¼ cup)	demerara (raw) sugar
50g	2 oz (¼ cup)	butter
3g	1 tsp	cinnamon
1g	¼ tsp	nutmeg
		2 eggs
60ml	2 fl oz (¼ cup)	milk

1. Break bread into small pieces and soak in cold water for at least 1 hour.

2. Strain and squeeze out water until it is as dry as possible.

3. Place into a bowl and crumble bread with your hands into tiny pieces.

4. Add the egg, butter and enough milk to enable the mixture to drop easily from a spoon. Add the dried fruit, sugar, and spices. Mix well.

5. Place into a greased baking tin 25cm x 35cm (9 in x 14 in). Bake in a preheated oven at 170°C /325°F/Gas Mark 3 for an hour or until slightly firm to the touch.

6. Serve warm with cream or custard.

Herbed crostini

These crispy snacks, also known as bruschetta, are wonderful on their own or topped with something fancy like smoked salmon or paté. These are typically made from old baguettes, but you can use any bread. Crostini can also be cut into smaller pieces and used as croutons in soups and salads.

Ingredients for 2 small loaves

Metric	Imperial/US	
		6 slices of stale bread
45ml	3 tbsp	olive oil
2.5g	½ tsp	basil and/or oregano
25g	1 oz	grated parmigiano (parmesan) cheese
1g	¼ tsp	sea salt

1. Slice old or stale bread into thin slices 1cm (½in) or less.

2. Brush generously with olive oil on both sides. Place on baking tray.

3. Sprinkle on salt, herbs and parmigiano cheese to taste.

4. Bake in a preheated oven at 180°C /350°F/ Gas Mark 4 for 8 to 12 minutes.

5. Serve warm from the oven.

BAKING GLUTEN FREE MADE EASY AND TASTY

Written by Julie Gritten, author of
My Family and Other Allergies

Allergies such as gluten and wheat intolerance have been on the rise since the latter part of the last century. More and more people are having gut health issues and cannot tolerate wheat or rye bread.

No known single cause has been found for this recent phenomenon. It may be a combination of pesticide residues, modern varieties of gluten rich wheat, recent yeast strains or baking methods. It has even been suggested that our current obsession with cleanliness has caused our gut flora to be depleted and that we may change this by getting a pet cat or dog or going to live on a farm. Whatever the cause, if you or your child suffer from wheat intolerance or have coeliac disease and can't tolerate gluten from oats or rye either, it isn't much help just knowing what causes it. Far better to find a way of eating without having to give up the deliciousness of baked goodies.

There are countries in the world which aren't as enamoured with wheat as we are. Tortilla in Mexico are made with cornmeal and arepas. In Colombia, Venezuela and Panama tortilla are made with masa harina, a kind of cornmeal which has been treated with lime powder. Ethiopian ingera are made with teff, which is their most common cereal crop.

Many different flours such as quinoa, soya, buckwheat (crepes in Brittany are made with buckwheat flour), sorghum, tapioca and brown rice are available in whole food shops in the UK. It is worth experimenting with these flours as they all have different flavours and textures. Companies like Doves Farm in Britain make good gluten-free (Gf) flour mixes for different purposes, from plain and self-raising white flours to brown bread flour.

We all love the idea of bread, toast and the smell of baking. Here are some tasty recipes for all, which are easy enough to be made with the help of a child. Older children, once they have had help with a recipe, can bake for themselves.

Though it might not be as successful as with gluten-breads, you can freeze most of these gluten-free breads if you freeze them as soon as they are cool but not yet hard. You can slice the Gf bread first with a clean, scalded knife if there is only one person in your household who eats Gf.

It is best not to think of these recipes as bread substitutes but rather as tasty baking goods in themselves, as baking Gf bread is not the same as baking gluten bread. Though there is no need to knead, this baking can still be great fun with children, involving chopping and mixing, setting aside to rise and testing the mixes. When baking with young children it is good to read the whole recipe and gather all the ingredients and equipment together before they begin to help. Older children who can read can help gather everything.

I've included some recipes which may not be actual bread but are fun, such as Irish farls, doughnuts and churros.

Blinis (no yeast)

Blinis are traditional Russian breads. Made for over a thousand years, now they have become a favourite wedding canapé, piled with smoked salmon and cream cheese.

You can make these with yeast as a raising agent as with traditional blinis. For a quick snack you can throw them together using any Gf flour, brown, white or buckwheat.

Ingredients for 6–8 blinis

METRIC	IMPERIAL/US	
100g	4 oz (1 cup)	Gf flour
60ml	2 fl oz (¼ cup)	milk or milk substitute
		salt and pepper
5g	2 tsp	bicarbonate of soda or baking powder
		or 1 tsp of quick yeast (in which case you
		must leave the mixture to bubble for 30 minutes)
100ml	4fl oz/(½ cup)	water, enough to mix to a smooth dropping texture
30ml	1fl oz/2 tbsp	oil for frying

1. Make a mix of all the ingredients, using enough water to make a smooth dropping consistency.

2. Brush the oil thickly in the frying pan and check its heat by dropping a tiny bit of batter into the oil and frying until it is golden brown.

3. Drop dessertspoonfuls of batter into the hot pan and fry on one side for about 2 minutes or until golden. Turn and fry the second side until golden.

4. Serve hot with soup or with honey for a quick sweet snack.

Brown loaves

Chia seeds are good fun. When they are put in water they form a jelly not unlike frogspawn, which invites lots of ribald comments from my littlest grandchildren.

Ingredients for 2 small loaves

METRIC	IMPERIAL/US	
15g	1 tbsp	chia seeds
100ml	4 fl oz (½ cup)	water
5g	½ tsp	salt
30ml	1 fl oz /2 tbsp	oil
150ml	5 fl oz (approx ½ cup)	milk or milk substitute
2.5ml	½ tsp	vinegar
5g	1 tsp	coconut sugar
250g	8 oz (2 cups)	brown bread Gf mix
10g	1 tbsp	quick yeast

1. Make a mix of the chia, water, oil, milk, vinegar and sugar and set to one side for 10 minutes.

2. Meanwhile in a large bowl make a mix of flour, salt and yeast. Make a well in the centre of the flour mix and pour in the wet ingredients.

3. Mix together until smooth, adding a little more milk if needed to form a thick dropping consistency. Pour into the two small well-oiled bread tins and leave for an hour or so until risen.

4. Preheat oven to 180°C/350° F/Gas Mark 4 and cook for 50-60 minutes.

5. Turn out onto a tray and allow to cool completely before slicing.

Churros

Chorros are originally from Portugal and Spain, taken to South America centuries ago. They are basically a street food of fried choux pastry served with a chocolate dip.

Ingredients for 4 people

Metric	Imperial/US	
45ml	1½ fl oz/3 tbsp	water
25g	1 oz/1 tbsp	sugar, plus 1 tbsp for coating
2.5g	¼ tsp	salt
30ml	1 fl oz/ 2 tbsp	sunflower oil
110g	4 oz (1 cup)	Gf flour
		oil for deep frying
5g	1 tsp	ground cinnamon

1. Combine the first four ingredients in a saucepan and bring to the boil. Remove from the heat, let it cool for a minute then stir in enough flour to form a soft dough.

2. At this stage it looks a bit weird. You can roll it in your fingers to form long sausage shapes or if you add less flour or a little more water it will be spoonable.

3. Heat the frying oil and drop a spoonful of mix into it – when it sizzles and rises to the surface the oil is hot enough.

4. Drop sausages or spoonfuls of mix into the hot oil in batches and fry until the churros are golden all over.

5. Drain on kitchen paper and roll in the sugar and cinnamon before serving, or drizzle with chocolate sauce.

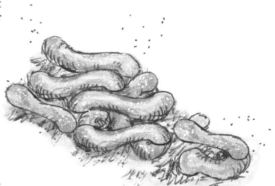

Focaccia flatbread

Focaccia (pronounced *fo-kah-cha*) is a traditional, Italian flatbread, made since ancient times. You can leave out the savoury toppings for a sweet bread.

Ingredients for one loaf

Metric	Imperial/US	
5g	2 tsp	quick yeast
250g	9 oz (2 cups)	Gf flour
2.5ml	½ tsp	xanthan gum
5g	½ tsp	sea salt
5g	½ tsp	sugar
100ml	3½ fl oz (½ cup)	warm milk or milk substitute
30ml	2 tbsp	extra virgin olive oil
30ml	2 tbsp	aquafaba (briny water from canned chickpeas)
1g	¼ tsp	baking soda
10ml	2 tsp	white wine vinegar

Topping

15g	1 tbsp	sliced olives
15ml	1 tbsp	olive oil
15g	1 tbsp	fresh rosemary leaves
2.5g	½ tsp	sea salt flakes

1. Sift together the flour, yeast, xanthan gum, and salt.

2. Mix the sugar and milk together in a bowl, add the oil and aquafaba and beat together. Beat into the flour mix to make a soft dough.

3. Mix the baking soda and white vinegar together to fizz then fold into the mixture. Using oiled hands, smooth the dough out into the oiled baking tray. Cover and keep warm for around 45 minutes until risen and puffy.

4. Preheat the oven to 190°C/375°F/Gas Mark 5.

5. Once the bread has doubled in size, poke fingertips into the dough to make indentations.

6. Drizzle with the olive oil and sprinkle with olives and rosemary leaves, and the sea salt flakes.

7. Bake for 30 minutes until the top is golden.

8. This is best eaten when fresh from the oven.

Irish farls

In Gaelic, *farl* means four parts. Traditionally, the dough is rolled into a circle which is cut into 4, then each round is flattened and cooked on a dry griddle or pan.

Ingredients for four farls

Metric	Imperial/US	
500g	16 oz (3½ cups)	floury potatoes
50g	2 oz (¼ cup)	butter or cooking oil
50g	2 oz (½ cup)	Gf plain flour plus extra for rolling out
1g	¼ tsp	salt
1.5g	¼ tsp	baking powder
		oil or butter for cooking

1. Cut the potatoes into slices and boil them in salty water until soft and tender. Mash them with the oil or butter and allow them to cool slightly.

2. In a large bowl sieve the flour together with the baking powder and salt. Add the warm mashed potatoes and work the mix gently to form a soft ball. Use a little more flour if it's too sticky or add milk if it's too dry.

3. Divide the dough into two halves. Roll out one half into a 15cm circle about 1cm thick. Cut it into quarters. Cook the four quarters in a frying pan with a little butter or oil for about 2 minutes each side.

4. Place on a warm plate and repeat with the other half of the dough.

5. Serve with eggs or smoked tofu and spinach, or straight from the pan with a little ketchup or sugar.

Pizza bases

Perfect for fussy eaters, this makes precooked bases for margherita type pizzas. You just need to add tomato sauce and grill with a cheese topping.

I use brown Gf flour for preference as white Gf flour sometimes has a cardboard like constancy when cooked this way.

Ingredients for 2x 25x30cm bases

METRIC	IMPERIAL/US	
200g	8 oz (2 cups)	Gf brown bread flour
5g	1 tsp	sugar
2.5g	½ tsp	ground nutmeg
1g	¼ tsp	salt
5g	2 tsp	quick dried yeast
20g	1 heaped tbsp	chia seed with 100ml water mix
100ml	3.5 fl oz (½ cup)	warm water
15ml	1 tbsp	olive oil
30ml	2 tbsp	oil for tins and hands

1. Oil two baking trays 25x30cm.

2. Sieve together the flour, yeast, salt, nutmeg and sugar. Mix the chia seed and water and allow to stand for 5 minutes.

3. Make a well in the centre of the flour mix and add the oil, chia mix and warm water. Mix well. Initially it will seem as if it won't come together. Mix a little more with oily hands.

4. At the point where it feels a little like play dough, divide the dough in half and spread both out on flat baking trays. Allow to rise until twice as thick and fluffy.

5. Bake for 30 minutes until golden. Spread with your favourite pizza sauce and grated cheese then place under a grill to toast.

Soda bread (sweet or savoury)

This makes a dense loaf with a great flavour. Especially good for toasting.

In hard water areas the addition of a teaspoon of lemon juice or vinegar will help the bread to rise.

I like a lot of soda in the bread, but if you find it too strong a taste try replacing the soda with just one teaspoon of bicarbonate or use two teaspoons of baking powder instead.

Ingredients for one loaf

METRIC	IMPERIAL/US	
300g	8 oz (2 cups)	brown Gf flour
100g	4 oz (1 cup)	buckwheat flour
5g	1 tsp	salt
10g	2 tsp	bicarbonate of soda
5g	1 tsp	caraway seeds* (optional)
15g	1 tbsp	chia seeds added to 4 tbsp of cold water
600ml	20 fl oz (2½ cups)	water

*replace the caraway seeds with 1 tbsp sugar and 1 tbsp raisins for a sweet version

1. Heat the oven to 200°C/400°F/Gas Mark 6.

2. Sieve together the flours, soda, salt and caraway seeds (or sugar and raisins). In a small bowl mix the chia with 4 tbsp of water and wait for a few minutes until it thickens up.

3. Add the chia mix to the 600ml of water and stir it all into the flour mix. Pour the mix into a well-oiled casserole pot with a close-fitting lid.

4. Bake in the hot oven for about 45 minutes until firm and golden brown.

5. Leave to cool a little before serving with savoury or sweet dishes.

Sweet potato and squash doughnuts

These are fun to make and so much tastier than commercial ones. This recipe needs adult supervision as it involves handling very hot, deep oil.

Ingredients for 12 doughnuts

METRIC	IMPERIAL/US	
125g	4½ oz (1 cup)	peeled and diced butternut squash
125g	4½ oz (1 cup)	peeled and diced sweet potato
5g	1 tsp	salt
5g	1 tsp	mixed spice
5g	2 tsp	instant dried yeast
250g	9 oz (2 cups)	Gf flour
		sunflower or coconut oil for deep frying
15g	1 tbsp	sugar
5g	1 tsp	ground cinnamon

1. Boil the squash and sweet potato chunks in a pan of boiling water for 10 to 15 minutes until soft, then drain and mash. Allow to cool.

2. In a large mixing bowl, combine the salt, mixed spice and yeast, then add the cooled pumpkin and sweet potato mash. Mix well and add enough of the flour to make a soft dough. Cover with a clean tea towel and set aside for 2 hours or until it has doubled in size.

3. Using floury hands, divide the dough into 20 even pieces, then form them into doughnut shapes and poke a large hole through the middle of each one. Leave to rise on a floured baking tray in a warm place for 10–15 minutes.

4. Meanwhile, heat the oil in a wok or deep frying pan and set the oven to a low temperature. Deep-fry the doughnuts for 4–5 minutes in batches until golden brown, turning once. Keep the cooked doughnuts in the warm oven until they are all done.

5. Mix the sugar and cinnamon together on a plate and roll the doughnuts in it until they are covered all over, then serve warm.

Chapter Five

Songs, poems and blessings to celebrate bread

A kitchen filled with songs and blessings enlivens not only the active hands of the baker, but transforms the quality of the bread itself. Children naturally love singing while their hands are busy. Singing lends strength to the rhythm of their hands while kneading dough, shaping the loaves or even cleaning up. It gives them energy and imagination to complete the task at hand.

The line between work and play dissolves as the playfulness of music helps to carry the work, making it less effort and more imaginative. People from traditional cultures sing while they are working for just this reason, with different songs for each different activity. Whether ploughing fields, sowing seeds, grinding grain or kneading bread, singing leavens all we do with joy.

Bread baked with love nourishes those who eat it every bit as much as it enlivens the baker. It is imprinted right into the loaves. Those who eat well-made bread are not only eating the substances flour, water, salt and yeast, they are eating the entire transformative process that has quite magically changed these earthy substances into living and life-giving sustenance. You can taste the difference!

Make your baking fun. Make it lively and imaginative, for this too will be a lasting part of the experience, and quite possibly the most significant part. Children know this instinctively and so can we.

Blessings, likewise, lighten the work of our hands by reminding us that baking bread is sacred work. They lift our hearts out of mundane realms and help us to see that the work we are doing is love made visible. Blessings can enhance our appreciation of the nourishment bread brings us, not only to give us a healthy physical body, but a rich soul and a lively and active spirit as well.

Prayers and blessings can be kneaded right into the dough and baked into every loaf. Dedicating bread in this way focuses the baker's attention on its spiritual role as the sustenance of life.

BREAD SONGS

Kneading song

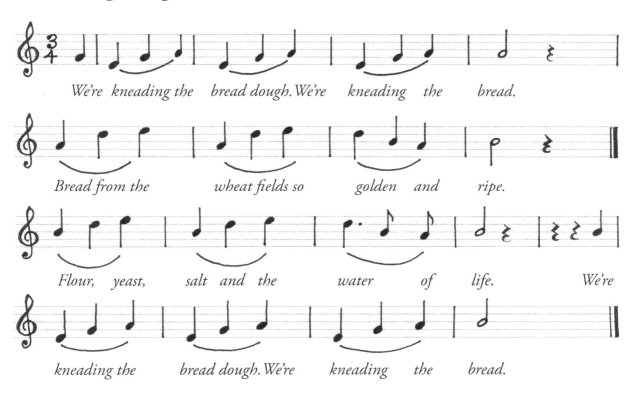

We're kneading the bread dough. We're kneading the bread.
Bread from the wheat fields so golden and ripe.
Flour, yeast, salt and the water of life. We're
kneading the bread dough. We're kneading the bread.

We're kneading the bread dough. We're kneading the bread.
Bread from the wheat fields so golden and ripe.
Flour, yeast, salt and the water of life.
We're kneading the bread dough, we're kneading the bread.

Kate Hammond

The song for the sickle

Cut the corn, cut the corn, Cut the corn ev-'ry morn',

Work all day, no rest or play, Ev-'ry day in the har-vest.

Cut the corn, cut the corn,
Cut the corn ev'ry morn',
Work all day, no rest or play,
Ev'ry day in the harvest.

Colin Price

Muffin man

Do you know the Muffin Man? The Muffin Man? The Muffin Man?

Do you know the Muffin Man? He lives on Drury Lane.

Do you know the Muffin Man?
The Muffin Man? The Muffin Man?
Do you know the Muffin Man?
He lives on Drury Lane.

Traditional

Oats, peas, beans and barley

Oats, peas, beans & barley grow Oats, peas, beans & barley grow Do you or I or an-y one know How oats, peas, beans & bar- ley grow?

Oats, peas, beans and barley grow
Oats, peas, beans and barley grow
Do you or I or anyone know
How oats, peas, beans and barley grow?

First the farmer sows the seed
Then he stands and takes his ease
He stamps his foot and claps his hands
And turns around to view the land!

Traditional French

Song of sixpence

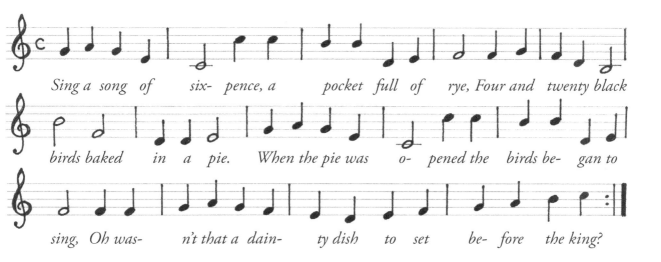

Sing a song of six- pence, a pocket full of rye, Four and twenty black

birds baked in a pie. When the pie was o- pened the birds be- gan to

sing, Oh was- n't that a dain- ty dish to set be- fore the king?

Sing a song of sixpence, a pocket full of rye,
Four and twenty blackbirds baked in a pie.
When the pie was opened the birds began to sing,
Oh wasn't that a dainty dish to set before the king?

The king was in his counting house counting out his money,
The queen was in the parlour eating bread and honey,
The maid was in the garden hanging out the clothes,
When down came a blackbird and pecked off her nose!

English nursery rhyme

A grace for meals

Bread is a lovely thing to eat.
God bless the barley and the wheat,
A lovely thing to breathe is air,
God bless the sunshine ev'ry where.
The earth is a lovely place to know,
God bless the folks that come and go.
Alive is a lovely thing to be.
Giver of life, we say, 'Bless Thee!'

Colin Price

Blessing on the bread

Ba- ruch a- ta A- don- ai el- o- he- nu melech ha-

o- lam ha- mot- zi le- chem min ha- a- a- retz.

A- a- men.

*Baruch ata Adonai elohenu melech ha-olam
hamotzi lechem min ha-aretz.
Amen.*

*Blessed be our God, king of the universe,
who has given us the grain of the earth.
Amen.*

Traditional Hebrew

For health and strength

For health & strength & dai- ly bread We praise thy name, oh Lord
Hal- le- lu- jah, Hal- le- lu- jah, Hal- le- lu- jah. A- men.

(round)

For health and strength and daily bread
We praise thy name oh Lord
Hallelujah, Hallelujah, Hallelujah.
Amen.

Traditional

The sun's blessing

Tis the bless-ing of the sun that has warmed the fields & brought forth the gold-en grain. Now the fields stand reaped of their gift of gold & we give thanks a-gain. But the leaves start fall-ing and the days grow cold And the earth is wrapped in mist. Let the win-ter come, for the sun has left in our hearts His gold- en gift.

'Tis the blessing of the sun that has warmed the fields
And brought forth the golden grain.
Now the fields stand reaped of their gift of gold
And we give thanks again.
But the leaves start falling and the days grow cold
And the earth is wrapped in mist.
Let the winter come, for the sun has left in our hearts
His golden gift.

Colin Price

Zum gali

Zum gali – gali – gali Zum gali – ga- li Zum gali – gali – gali Zum

Zum. Let us sing with joy as we work. Let us work with joy as we sing.

(round)

Zum gali – gali – gali
Zum gali – gali
2x
Zum gali – gali – gali
Zum.

Let us sing with joy as we work. 2x
Let us work with joy as we sing.

Traditional Hebrew

Hot cross buns

Hot cross   buns!   Hot   cross   buns!   One a penny,   two a penny. Hot cross buns!

If you have no daughters, give them to your sons. One a penny, two a penny.

Hot   cross   buns!

Hot cross buns! Hot cross buns!
One a penny, two a penny. Hot cross buns!
If you have no daughters, give them to your sons. One a
penny, two a penny. Hot cross buns!

Traditional

John Barleycorn

There were three men come out of the west Their for- tunes for to

try And these three men made a solemn vow John Bar- ley

corn should die. They ploughed, they sow- ed, they harr-owed him,

in, Threw clods up- on his head And these three men

made a sol- emn vow John Bar- ley- corn was dead.

There were three men come out of the west
Their fortunes for to try
And these three men made a solemn vow
John Barleycorn should die.
They ploughed, they sowed, they harrowed him in,
Threw clods upon his head
And these three men made a solemn vow
John Barleycorn was dead.

They let him lie for a very long time
Till the rain from heaven did fall
Then Little Sir John sprung up his head
And so amazed them all.
They let him stand till midsummer
Till he grew both pale and wan
Then Little Sir John grew a long sharp beard
And so became a man.

They hired men with the scythes so sharp
To cut him off at the knee
They rolled him and tied him about the waist
And used him barbarously.
They hired men with the sharp pitchforks
To pierce him to the heart
And the loader he served him worse than that
For he tied him to a cart.

They wheeled him around and around the field
Till they came unto a barn
And there they made a solemn mow
Of poor John Barleycorn.
They hired men with the crab-tree sticks
To strip him skin from bone
And the miller he treated him worst of all
For he ground him between two stones.

Here's Little Sir John in a nut-brown bowl
And brandy in a glass
And Little Sir John in the nut-brown bowl
Proved the stronger man at last.
For the huntsman, he can't hunt the fox
Nor loudly blow his horn
And the tinker can't mend kettles or pots
Without a little of the Barleycorn.

Traditional English

145

Shortnin' Bread

Three little child-ren lyin' in bed   Two was sick and the   other most dead.

Sent for the doc-tor, the doc- tor   said: Feed those children on   short- nin'   bread.

Mammy's little baby loves shortnin', shortnin'   Mammy's little baby loves shortnin' bread.

Three little children lyin' in bed.
Two was sick and the other most dead.
Sent for the doctor, the doctor said:
Feed those children on shortnin' bread.

Mammy's little baby loves shortnin', shortnin'
Mammy's little baby loves shortnin' bread.
2x

Put on the skillet, put on the lid
Mammy goin' to bake a little shortnin' bread
That ain't all she's goin' to do
Mammy goin' to make a little coffee too.

Mammy's little baby loves shortnin', shortnin'
Mammy's little baby loves shortnin' bread.
2x

Traditional Southern USA

SOUL FOOD

I have baked for communities large and small, sometimes with assistants as young as four years of age. I remember baking and serving fresh bread for a conference of 120 people. The mood in the kitchen was especially festive. We were working well together, singing and thoroughly enjoying our tasks, and one another. We filled the kitchen with our music and purposeful activity.

The bread we baked – some Italian loaves with herbs –turned out especially light and flavourful. They were not exceptional by a baker's standards, but the way they were received by the guests was notable. The guests went straight for the bread and kept on asking for more and more. They literally sang its praises until there were only crumbs left. It seemed that they could taste the joy of our young bakers and craved more of this complete nourishment.

Time and again I have noticed a similar phenomenon. Other chefs have confirmed that whenever the mood in the kitchen is light and gay, so too is the bread. Likewise, when the mood is heavy, somehow the bread just won't rise or taste right. Joy-filled bread nourishes the baker as well as the consumer in ways that go far beyond the nutrients of the ingredients. It has become soul food, with joy as the chef's secret ingredient.

Before the flour, the mill
Before the mill, the grain
The sun, the earth, the rain
The beauty of God's will.

Origin unknown

From *Prayers and Graces* with kind
permission of Floris Books

First the farmer sows the seed
Then he stands and takes his ease
He stamps his foot and claps his hands
And turns around to view the land!

Traditional French

Bread

Bread is good for us to eat
It gives us warmth.
It gives us light.
It gives us strength.
It gives us life.
As it is given to us
Out of love.

Erika Grantham

For sun and rain

For sun and rain
For grass and grain
For all who toil on sea and soil
That we may eat our daily bread
We give our loving thanks to you.

Unknown

Blow wind blow

Blow wind blow
And go mill go
That the miller may grind the corn
That the baker may take it
And into bread bake it
And bring us a loaf in the morn
Bring us a loaf in the morn.

Unknown

We break this bread together with hearts aware
Not bread alone, but God's life and love we share.

A.C. Harwood

Blessings

May God bless our daily bread
So that our souls with life be fed.

Unknown

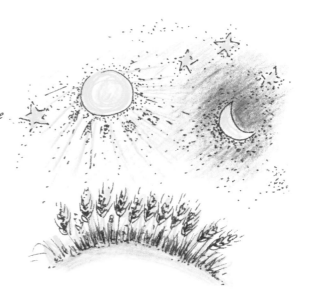

> *Blessed be thou Lord, God of the Universe*
> *Who brings forth bread from the Earth*
> *And makes glad the hearts of men.*
>
> Hebrew blessing

Earth who gives to us this food
Earth who gives to us this food
Sun who makes it ripe and good
Dear Sun, dear Earth
By you we live
To you our loving thanks we give.

Christian Morgenstern

From *Prayers and Graces* with kind permission of Floris Books

To gratitude

To the sun above
And the Earth below
To the wind that blows
And the water that flows
To the patient farmer who lovingly sows
And all that graciously grows…
Thank you!

Warren Lee Cohen

Gardening verse

Here we stand, upon God's land
Holding forth our willing hands
All our strength and love we give
That all Earth's creatures in peace may live.

We will work, and till the earth,
Thanking God for this, our birth
Head and heart and hands, we pray
Be our gift in life this day.

Julie Barrett

Grace over the meal
Substance of Earth
Essence of light
Grace of heaven
In us unite.

Francis Edmunds

From *Prayers and Graces* with kind permission
of Floris Books

All things bright and beautiful
All things bright and beautiful, all creatures great and small
All things wise and wonderful, the Lord God made them all.

Each little flower that opens, each little bird that sings
God made their glowing colours, God made their tiny wings.

Cecil Frances Alexander

Playing with bread
Be bread.
Drab bard, abed, bored.
Dare!
Dare! Be brae.
Dare dear Reb!
Dare!
Be bread!

Beverley McCartney

Betty Botter

Betty Botter bought some butter
But, she said, the butter's bitter
If I put it in my batter
It will make my batter bitter
But a bit of better butter
Will make my batter better.
So she bought a bit of butter
Better than her bitter butter,
And she put it in her batter
And the batter was not bitter.
So 'twas better Betty Botter
Bought a bit of better butter.

Tongue twister

Pat a cake

Pat a cake, pat a cake, baker's man
Bake me a cake as fast as you can
Pat it and prick it and mark it with a 'B'
And put it in the oven for Baby and me.

English nursery rhyme

A soul cake

A soul, a soul, a soul cake
Please good masters a soul cake
An apple, a pear, a plum or a cherry
Four good things to make you all merry
A soul, a soul, a soul cake
Please good masters a soul cake.

English nursery rhyme

Buried in the earth, a kernel of wheat
Is transformed into tall stalks of grain.
Crushed in the mill, its value increases
And it becomes bread, invigorating to the soul.
Ground in the teeth, it becomes spirit, mind, and the understanding of reason
Lost in Love, that spirit delights the sower's after the sowing.

Rumi

Dragon Baked Bread

The bubbles did burst then blow once more
And billow and swell and burp and snore…
It gurgled and bubbled and spurted to life.
It grew by the minute no matter the strife.
It rose, it swelled, it puffed like the moon.
It would swallow the whole palace, ever so soon.

Warren Lee Cohen, from *Dragon Baked Bread*

Chapter Six

Bread projects and educational activities

Building a bread oven

Wood-fired bread ovens invite a child's natural curiosity to explore the relationship between fire and the food we eat. A wood-fired bread oven makes the whole process of baking bread visible. Wood needs to be gathered and fires built. Flames glow inside the oven as smoke wafts out. And, fire imposes its own safety discipline. The oven hearth takes the magic of baking to another level, where fire transforms yeast, flour and water into golden brown bread, a mouth-watering delight.

I have had fun building bread ovens with students in many countries around the world including UK, USA, Canada and Madagascar. A few years ago, I worked with a high school class in Hereford U.K. to build a bread oven and enclosure for their school's kindergarten. We designed the oven, gathered materials, discussed all the details, and built it in a week of afternoons.

The students dug clay from a nearby riverbank and kneaded it to the right consistency with their feet. The kindergarten children enjoyed watching us working and helped out where they could. This was their oven and they wanted to join in. With the help of two parents, we completed the oven, landscaped the garden and then lit some small drying-out fires. This was a true community building project that brought together parents, teachers, teenagers and young children all inspired by good bread.

Now the kindergarten teacher relates: 'We fire our kindergarten bread oven every Friday. I light the fire first thing in the morning so its warm glow greets the children as they arrive. The children help me knead the dough and then later to shape little buns for our snack. When we put the risen buns into the oven there is a moment of silent, magical anticipation. We wait and wait and wait. And, at last the buns are done, perfect with butter and honey. What a perfect way to end our week together.'

Wood-fired bread ovens can be a beautiful addition to any garden or school play yard. They can be designed to fit into the landscape or as a sculpted addition to any stone or brick outbuildings, or other structures already in place. They can be simple domes or sculpted into animals, dragons or other natural shapes. These are wonderful projects to work on, as children and adults can be involved in so many steps in the process, from design and construction right down to baking hearth loaves. Every aspect is meaningful work, and everyone can contribute in some way. Many hands make light work.

Wood-fired earthen ovens have been used round the world to bake bread. Although each country has its own design, the principles of construction are the same. Inexpensive local materials are used to hold the heat efficiently, long enough to bake pizza, bread, casseroles, cakes, potatoes or pumpkin and…. That's it. All it takes is some earth, clay and straw. Even a chimney is not necessary, but an extra detail.

It is not surprising that building bread ovens is proving a popular project in schools and communities. Wood-fired bread ovens are increasingly used in regular bread baking or pizza nights. Perhaps there is a need for one in your community. Here is a basic outline of how to go about it from my experience of building them with children and adults in schools, communities and private homes. Just as with dough, once you get the feel for the earthen cob mixture, the rest flows much more easily. For further information, please see the bibliography at the back of this book.

12 steps to building and firing your own earthen bread oven

1. Choose a site

You first want to select the best site to build your bread oven. Beware of overhanging trees which may suffer from the heat of the fire.

Your oven will need a roof to keep it dry otherwise the earth and clay that make up your oven will melt away in the rain. It is best if the site is not too far from your kitchen work area, as you will have to carry many things back and forth. Design your oven to meet your baking needs and the aesthetics of the site. I have found that an oven floor plan of approximately 60cm x 90cm (2 ft x 3 ft) is a good average size for a home or school. The inner, working dimensions of the oven will actually be smaller due to the thickness of the oven walls. Check the local wind and weather patterns. Ovens work best if the prevailing wind is not blowing directly into the oven opening, and no one wants too much smoke blowing into their home.

2. Lay a foundation

Build a foundation out of bricks, block, stone or earth to raise the oven to waist height.

This foundation can be functional and/or artistic and serves to make the oven easier to load and unload. Put a layer of sand at least 2cm (1 in) thick on top of the foundation. If the sand will not stay on top of the foundation, then hold it in place with a little perimeter wall made from cob (described in step 5). Smooth and level the sand with a board. Lay firebricks (the hard bricks used to line chimneys) on the sand bed, to make a level floor for the oven. You can use regular building bricks, but these will not last as long. The bricks rest on top of the sand without mortar and can simply be replaced if any of them crack.

3. Make a door

Cut out a wooden door from hardwood (oak, ash, maple) 30cm x 25cm x 4cm (12 in x 10 in x 1½in), preferably rounded at the top. Make a handle for the door. Most of my doors have been made from oak and have lasted many firings over several years. But if you want your door to be even more durable, line the inside with sheet metal cut to fit the door.

4. Create a temporary sand form

Build a sand dome directly on the oven floor using sharp or builders' sand. Water helps the sand keep its shape, so that you can get straight vertical walls. Spray it occasionally with water if needed. Use wooden boards to smooth and scrape the form until it is the shape you want and nice and solid. A good height to aim for is 45cm (18 in) or 1½times the height of the door. This sand form is temporary and will be dug out after the earthen oven has been constructed around it.

5. Knead clay, straw and sand

Now we are getting to the fun bit that takes plenty of energy and allows people to get healthily dirty. Most soil has clay in it. If there is not much at your site, you can either dig it from somewhere else or use pottery clay. Ideally the earth should have about 25% clay, but I have had success building ovens using pottery clay mixed with plenty of grog (ground up bits of fired pottery), sand and straw.

In general I mix 5 shovels of clay/earth with one shovel of straw cut to 10cm (4 in) lengths and 1 shovel of sand. Straw gives the mixture tensile strength while sand reduces the amount of shrinkage. The mixture is now called cob, and its make-up varies from one site to another. It should be malleable, stiff and consistently mixed. It is always best to make a few small test bricks and see how strong they are when dry, and which have the fewest cracks. You should be able to stand on a dried cob brick without it crumbling under your weight. Remember this mixture was the first 'concrete'. Buildings around the world are made out of cob, some standing for many hundreds of years. There is even a cob apartment building 9 stories tall in Yemen. It can be a strong and durable building material.

Then with bare feet, or rubber boots if the weather is cold, stomp on the cob until it becomes evenly mixed. Use as little extra water as possible to facilitate even mixing. Too much water makes the mix sloppy and weak and takes forever to dry.

Once you get in the mood of things, cob can feel really nice squishing between your toes. Kneading the cob with your feet is a real workout. Find a good

working rhythm. If you do this on top of an old plastic tarpaulin then it is easier to turn the mixture over periodically to help make it uniform. When it is well mixed, break off loaf-sized chunks and further knead these with your hands. The oven itself is made just like bread by carefully kneading the cob (earth, sand and straw) into bricks.

6. Build cob igloo

Take these kneaded loaves of earthen cob and place them around the base of the sand oven form. Complete the first layer all the way around the sand form, joining each loaf of cob to its neighbours. Continue to build up around the form layer by layer from bottom to top. Pinch, press and poke the different loaves together as you go until you have made a lumpy igloo that covers the entire sand mound. You have completed the first of 2 layers that make the oven walls.

Place the wooden door on the front of the oven, flush with the cob igloo. Keep the door vertical and push it into the cob until the entire door is pressed against this first layer of cob. In a few days, after the cob igloo dries, you will remove the door and cut an opening into the oven (see step 8). Now add a second layer of cob built up from the base to the top in the same manner. Join new bricks to each other as well as to the inner layer. You are aiming to make one monolithic cob dome.

Make sure that the arch over the door is strong and well-moulded. Oven walls should be anywhere from 7cm to 20cm (3 in to 8 in) thick. This can be easily tested with a stick poked into the cob walls. The thicker the walls, the more heat they will hold, but the longer they will take to heat up.

7. Sculpt oven

Make sure that the cob dome has no air pockets in it. Using a short length of wooden board, hit the cob oven all over its surface. This helps to strengthen the connections between bricks and to remove any pockets of trapped air.

Now you can either leave the oven an elegant dome or sculpt it into an interesting shape.

Simply add on more cob and/or carefully carve into the outer layer to create the desired form. These ovens do not need a chimney and in fact work better if the only opening is the door. However, an external chimney (i.e. not one in the back of the oven) in front of the door helps keep smoke away from the pizza chef. I have used cardboard forms to make an external front chimney, around which I build up layers of cob. It only needs to be strong enough to hold the cob in place until it dries. The cardboard is later removed or burned out.

8. Remove the sand form and carve door opening

Depending on the weather, the oven dome can take a day, week or month to dry. Be patient – a slowly-dried oven will tend to have fewer cracks and last longer. When the outside of the oven gets leather hard, then it is safe to remove the sand form from within. The cob can now support itself, but treat the oven gently at this point.

Remove the wooden door and cut an opening into the oven using an old kitchen knife. Make this opening slightly smaller than the door so that the oven forms a good seal with the door on both its front and side edges. Gently scrape out all the sand. You can use this sand for your next project. If there are any large cracks or gaps in the oven, these can be filled with extra cob mixture.

9. Dry with small fires

When you are satisfied with the shape of your oven, you can begin to help it to dry.

Patience at this point will reduce the number and size of future cracks, but do not worry. Most of my ovens have some cracks and none have ever fallen to pieces as a result. Start with small fires built in different parts of the oven to help it dry evenly. This can be a good time to start gathering wood for the bread baking to come, and practice lighting fires with small pieces of kindling.

10. Fire the oven

When at last the oven is dry, it is time to fire the oven. I have heard of ovens built for festivals that are fired on the same day they are finished. This works well enough for a short period of time, but rapid drying does shorten an oven's useful life. I prefer to let mine dry out more slowly over about a month. It all depends on the local weather and your needs.

Start a fire towards the front of the oven and within easy reach, using dry, untreated, unpainted wood. Once the fire is burning, add more wood towards the rear of the oven, so that the fire burns deeper and deeper into the oven. This way the flames heat the entire oven. The door should be off and will only be used later when loaves of bread are baking in the oven.

The door opening serves as both air inlet and exhaust. Cold air comes into the oven at the base of the door opening, while hot exhaust leaves through the upper part. You can, very carefully, feel the warm and cold air with your hand. Once the oven is hot, watching the flames dance inside can be entrancing. Firing an oven up to baking temperature requires anywhere between 2 to 4 hours. It is better to allow the oven to get a little too hot and then have to cool it down, than have uncooked bread sitting in an oven that is too cool.

11. Prepare the bread and oven to bake

When baking yeasted bread, I usually start the bread dough just after lighting the oven. This way the loaves of bread are perfectly risen just as the oven reaches the right baking temperature.

It is a little different with sourdough. I begin my sourdough bread the night before baking it. The next morning I knead and shape the loaves and then light a fire in the oven. I like to say a little blessing on the oven as the first flames take: that this fire may bring health to all who participate in baking and eating this bread. It has become a cherished part of the experience.

When the oven is hot to the touch on the outside, it is usually hot enough to bake on the inside. Here trial and error is the only aid because each oven behaves so differently.

Scrape out all the ashes into a metal bin or bucket using a garden hoe. Then damp mop the bottom of the oven to get the last of the ashes cleaned out. The mopping will both clean the oven and cool the oven floor so that the bottom of the bread will not burn.

To determine proper oven temperature you can use an oven thermometer, test with your hand as traditional bakers do, or use the 'flour test' in which you toss some white flour onto the oven's brick floor. If the flour burns in less than 10 seconds, the oven is too hot. If it turns golden brown, then it is just right. You will get the feel for this once you have used your oven a few times.

12. And bake bread!

Place the loaves directly on the oven floor leaving 2 to 5cm (1 to 2 in) for expansion between the loaves. An oven peel made from wood or metal can be helpful to load and remove the bread. Once the oven is loaded, spray the loaves with water to help give them a crisp and flavourful crust. Immediately place the oven door over the opening, to seal in the moisture. Wait. Spray twice again at 5 and 10 minutes. If some parts of the oven are hotter than others then you will need to rotate the loaves. Wait, wait and in less time than an indoor oven, the loaves will be baked. Use the finger thump test and listen for a hollow sound. Let the loaves cool and admire them. They are unlike anything that you can create in an indoor oven – a crusty masterpiece!

Building a bread oven with a high school class in Hereford UK

Bakery and farm

> '*What I remember most vividly from school is when we did things. I can clearly remember when we made feta cheese in the classroom sink. We went to the school garden and picked fresh tomatoes, snow peas and lettuce and then made a salad with our homemade feta. It was the best salad I ever ate.*'
>
> *A biodynamic farming student*

This story, like so many childhood memories I have heard, supports the idea that people are more likely to remember things they did themselves. Children learn by doing. The more they participate in an activity, such as tending a garden, baking bread or making cheese, the deeper the impression. I believe giving children a solid foundation of lifetime skills, confidence and knowledge is the highest aim of child rearing and education.

Visiting a farm or a bakery can leave a similarly profound impression. Many farms and bakeries welcome families with children and school groups. If they don't advertise such visits, it is worth asking. The Soil Association has a network of working farms that are open to the public. Please see the bibliography for useful websites.

We are so disconnected from an agrarian lifestyle that children will naturally be filled with questions and want to know what everything does and how it all works.

Whether it is meeting the farmer, the baker, the animals or the machines, children cannot help but be affected by how much care and attention has been given so that everything turns out well.

Some farms and bakeries will even let the children join in. What a profound memory working with the farmer or baker can create for children! Here is a person who dedicates his or her energy towards nurturing others in practical ways, tending the land, cultivating our food and harvesting it. Without this hard work, we might starve. One farmer told me of her encounter with a teenager from London, who, upon seeing a carrot being harvested from the ground for the first time, said, 'I always thought that carrots came from trees'.

> *Patrick Holden, an organic farmer, remembers: 'I had a suburban upbringing in and around London but when I was five years old my mother took me to visit a dairy farm in Essex. I remember standing in the traditional cow shed, with sweet smelling animals being milked into stainless steel churns. The experience left a lasting impression – so much so that I ended up establishing an organic dairy farm in west Wales.*'

Secret message buns

There is a lovely story of a baker who liked to write notes to himself on bits of paper, fragments of his daily musings. One of these happened to fall into the dough. A customer found this accidental note in her bread and was so impressed with the baker's wisdom that she asked him to bake a batch of buns for a party she was giving, with a note in each. Soon more and more people wanted these special buns with the baker's notes inside them. Not only was his bread sustaining but so was his wisdom (see Jacob the Baker in the bibliography).

Secret message buns can be a wonderful way to make and share messages with people you care about. These can be Valentine's Day messages, clues for a treasure hunt, numbered parts of a longer story, or just thoughtful insights that surprise the person who finds them in a bun.

To make secret message buns, simply write a note on a thin strip of paper.

- Fold this strip with the ink (non-toxic) on the inside.
- Prepare any bread dough as usual.
- When it is time to shape the buns, press a note inside each one.
- Let them rise and bake as usual.
- Make sure to let people know so they do not try to eat the paper by mistake.

Sculptures and decorations

Nearly any shape can be sculpted out of bread, either from one loaf or by joining several together with wooden skewers.

Animals are particularly fun for children to make, as are imaginative elements from stories, such as dragons. I have enjoyed working with children making human shapes, as well as dogs, cats, birds, fish, flowers, spider webs, the alphabet and more. There is no end to where their creativity can take

them. Nuts, seeds and raisins can be added for extra details.

You can make shapes several ways: by piecing together many little bits (balls, strands, braids) of dough, by pinching or cutting into loaves before you put them into the oven, or, for larger constructions, by assembling baked loaves with wooden skewers. The forms always tend to get a bit puffy as the dough is always rising in all directions. This is why I do the final forming (pinching, stretching or cutting) right before I put the loaves in the oven. I generally use baking sheets to bake these shapes in the oven. Make sure to grease all the baking surfaces well and to allow for plenty of rising/expansion in the forms. Sometimes I use heat-resistant forms such as an upturned metal bowl to help construct, say a hat or a boat.

Sometimes I like to explore the contrasting qualities of bread dough and ceramic clay. Bread dough is so warm and alive. It literally pushes back when you try to form it and resists all of your efforts to shape it. Clay on the other hand is cold and stays completely still. It waits for your impulse and receives every gesture you imprint on it including your bodily warmth and moisture. It literally sucks these away from your skin. Clay is completely receptive, whereas bread dough is much more expansive, with its own agenda. They are completely opposite in their natures, the yin and yang of sculptural media. The capacities needed to form each material challenge different parts of the artist's sensitivity and creativity. The results also give quite a different feeling of satisfaction.

Baking challenges

Once your children have learned how to bake bread and know how to follow a recipe, why not give them other challenges to develop their creativity and resourcefulness?

1. Give individual or pairs of children the same ingredients and recipe each to guide them. Challenge them to see who can make the highest standing bread loaf without using a tin. They can explore what makes loaves rise and are bound to discover many other things in the process.

2. Start new sourdough cultures with a group of children. Each child or team can choose its own recipe of grains to make the most active and flavourful culture. Observe them daily and compare their similarities and differences. After 10 days they should be ready to leaven loaves. Which one(s) work best? If you have a microscope, you can observe the yeast and bacteria in action.

3. Invite individual children or groups of children to invent their own bread recipes using the ingredients you have in your home, classroom and/or garden. Compare the different qualities of the breads they make and celebrate each one's best attributes. Make sure that the available ingredients include some form of raising agent: yeast, sourdough, baking powder or baking soda otherwise their results are likely to be better for building than for eating.

4. Baking bread can be leaven for the imagination and stimulate creativity. After making bread with children, why not encourage them to write a story or poem about bread?

Chapter Seven

Enlivening the senses – teaching with bread

Many children today lack the opportunity to play freely and exercise. They spend more and more time immobilised in car seats or in front of televisions and computers. Too much sitting in one place is bad for adults, let alone children, who need lots of movement in their early years to develop their senses of coordination and balance. These essential skills need to be exercised time and time again. By using their senses children come to know and trust in these tools for living in the world.

Research shows that until basic sensory experiences are met, a child finds it difficult to move on to other developmental stages. If sensory capacities are poorly developed, children can struggle at home and school. They are held back, their natural abilities hampered. Don't worry if you feel you or your children have missed out on an essential developmental stage. While it may take a bit more effort to develop in later life, it is never too late to work on developing human capacities.

The activity of baking, and eating, bread exercises many of these developing sensory capacities in children. The warm bread dough gives children's hands a natural resistance and massages their most sensitive areas. As they work with the dough, the dough is working on them. This rhythmic exercise with their muscles brings a warm and healthy flush to children's faces. They feel vibrant and alive. They soon notice the fragrant smell of fresh bread as it fills the whole house.

The golden crust delights their eyes. If they listen carefully, they can hear little crackling noises as it cools. All of these experiences combine to make the mouth water and the tummy yearn for a bite.

Once the bread has cooled, here at last is the long-anticipated taste, with the satisfaction of eating something this good, made by children's own hands. This feeling defies description. Bread truly is a feast for the senses that delights and tantalises them through the whole process of kneading, baking, waiting and eating. By senses, I mean not only the five senses of touch, taste, smell, sight and hearing. There are other equally important senses and qualities as well, such as balance, coordination and proportion. I have found the human developmental research, inspired by the work of Rudolf Steiner, helpful in a broader understanding of the senses and their development.

Steiner's observations led to the view that human beings have 12 senses which evolve at their individual pace. The physical senses, touch, well-being, movement and balance are the first to develop in early childhood. Then come the soul senses, smell, taste, sight and warmth, which come into their own during adolescence with the aid of the physical senses. Last to develop are what Steiner calls the senses of individuality, the ones that help to perceive your own unique self as well as other people's. These mature only in adulthood. All of these 12 senses are human capacities that require one another for their healthy development. Each one is interrelated with the others and is vital for healthy development.

A baby first develops the physical senses. The sense of touch tells him where the boundaries of his body are, how there is a world not part of him and he is separate. A baby feels well (or not) with his whole body. He is either cooing or crying, and the whole body is involved. Babies are in a constant state of movement, which they only gradually become aware of. And the sense of balance comes a little later, as they find their relationship to gravity with crawling, sitting and eventually walking. These four physical senses must first develop healthily. Once the four physical senses have come into their own, they then serve as a strong foundation for the rest. Young children need to exercise, explore and test them time and again. The activity of baking bread by hand can be such a wonderful stimulus for these senses.

The twelve senses according to Rudolf Steiner

Physical senses	Soul senses	Individuality senses
Balance	Warmth	Another person
Movement	Sight	Thought/concept
Well-being	Taste	Word
Touch	Smell	Hearing

The human hand

Let me explain more about the importance of developing our abilities by taking a look at the human hand. It combines both strength and sensitivity to do a huge variety of functions including threading a needle, playing the piano and building a home. It can grip, hold, pinch, pat, stroke or knead. Hands are full of expression, from the way we gesture, to a person using sign language. How do our hands fulfil their functionality, dexterity and expression? Each part of the hand needs a host of different challenges and a variety of exercises to awaken and develop to its full potential and usefulness.

Kneading bread dough can do just that. It exercises and massages the whole hand. In a gentle and rhythmic way, it fosters manual circulation, fine muscle development as well as attuned fine and gross motor coordination. It stimulates healthy development and awareness of the palm, fingers and the entire surface and structure of the hand, even between the fingers where the dough inevitably reaches. Sensitivity arises as each part of the hand is employed to shape the dough into loaves.

Traditional Chinese medicine, in common with Steiner's research, sees the human being in a holistic way, with every part connected to each other.

According to Chinese medicine, the palms of our hands are the nexus of many of the body's meridian lines that connect with the rest of the body. Massaging a ball of dough with your palms naturally stimulates these meridian points and thus many of the body's other organs which are connected along these energetic meridian lines, especially the heart. We really must start to see the human being as a whole and interconnected being, not as a collection of isolated parts, as is the tendency in western medicine.

While we knead bread dough, the dough also kneads us. Working with dough exercises the upper body. The rhythmic motion of kneading soon finds a harmony with your breathing. Heart, lungs and hands become united in a common motion. There is warmth in the dough, in your energetic kneading and, of course, from the oven, and these engender a sense of growing vitality. You are warming to the task, which warms you. This brings its own sense of well-being. When your whole body is moving purposefully in rhythm, you cannot help but feel healthy and alive.

Baking bread gives children the opportunity to practice other vital mental and social capacities that are equally essential for healthy living. These include:

Active thinking, sensing
- judging proportion
- judging size
- mental figuring
- logical sequencing
- problem solving

Life attributes
- patience
- wholeness – appreciation of nature's interdependent relationships
- meaningfulness
- contribution to others
- joy

when using measuring cups for liquids, as well as scales for weighing dry ingredients. Young bakers also learn about sequencing for baking: when to light the oven so that it is ready at the same time as the dough, when to add the other ingredients and how to best use the time while the bread is rising. This juggling with choices to get the right outcome can help them organise and structure their own lives.

When things don't go according to plan, children have to call on strategic thinking. So often we don't have the right size pans or the exact ingredients, or we accidentally add too much of something. Learning to make mathematical adjustments sharpens a child's sense of mental figuring. Searching for another size pan or substitutes for missing ingredients helps a child take an active part in problem solving. Children gain so much with a bit of practice. They also learn from any mistakes so support them if this happens. Coping with challenges gives them the fortitude to deal with the bigger ones later on.

Following recipes is a great way to teach a child many different ways of thinking. Reading through the step-by-step instructions is a learning tool in itself. Not only do children practice their reading skills (if they are of the age to read by themselves) but they also become acquainted with the laws of proportion, balance and measurement. They practice accuracy

Numbers

Recipes require a familiarity with numbers and fractions. In fact, many children first encounter fractions when using a recipe to cook. Using numbers in a practical context gives figures a whole new meaning and helps ground a child's understanding in concrete ways. Further lessons with mathematics can be created by doubling, tripling or halving a recipe or in converting it from metric to imperial units. These are pleasant problems to pose children as they have potentially delicious consequences.

When I was teaching children about fractions and later decimals, we did a lot of baking. This gave us the practical experience of solving the problems on paper, and testing our results in the mixing bowl. Children tasted the dough to see whether our calculations were correct. Besides involving many of the children's senses, cooking with fractions had the tangible reward of something satisfying to eat. The children looked forward to these mathematics classes – they were a treat and everyone was able to grasp (and taste) how they worked.

At the end of our lessons on fractions, I asked the children, 'Would you prefer to have ⅛th of the pizza or ⅐ th of the pizza?' By this time, their instinct for numbers was so developed that they knew, without having to work it out, that ⅐ th was the larger piece – and that is what they asked for.

Chapter Eight

Baking at school

Baking bread can be an engaging and educational activity for children of all ages, but it does take some planning and preparation to fit it into a busy school schedule. This chapter gives practical ideas for how to incorporate baking into the curriculum at all levels to meet children's different developmental needs.

It is important to check food hygiene regulations which have been enacted to ensure safe and sanitary conditions when handling food. Your local authority will have the information you need to avoid any problems.

Equipment

- oven (even a small table top oven or a convection oven will work)
- clean countertop or table preferably at waist height for children
- sink for washing hands and dishes, sponge and soap
- large mixing bowl
- wooden spoon
- measuring scale, cups and spoons
- bread tins or trays
- plastic or beeswax wrap
- dustpan and brush

Optional

- rolling pin
- apron
- hat
- cooling rack
- pastry knife
- sharp knife
- metal grater
- juicer
- flexible scraper
- pastry brush
- an assortment of smaller bowls and jars to store frequently used ingredients

Sure Start and preschool
Activity time – 1 hour

In the early years, bread dough is best used for its tactile appeal. Children enjoy playing with the warm springy dough and making little buns to eat. If any dough falls on the floor, then set it aside as play dough that can be worked and worked by energetic hands. It is wonderful exercise for their developing hands, arms, and all of their senses as mentioned in the previous chapter. The baking session will go most smoothly if the dough is prepared ahead of time and not too sticky. Try the easy white bread recipe (page 56), adding extra flour as needed.

Show the children how to knead the dough by doing it right there in front of them as children learn best through imitation. Sit around a low table if you can. Then give each child a mouse-sized ball of dough that has been dipped in flour to keep from sticking. Let them be to roll it, flatten it and play with it to their hearts' content. After 10 minutes or more put their creations on a greased baking tray. Let them rise until doubled in size. Bake as you would small buns for 10 to 12 minutes at 190°C /375°F/Gas Mark 5.

Kindergarten
Activity time – 1 to 2½ hours

Kindergarten children are even more capable and eager to participate in baking bread. It is wonderful to let them witness a process from start to finish. Even if they do not do much of the work, they will be nurtured just being in a baking environment. It teaches them in a most practical and subtle way how human effort can transform the gifts of nature into delicious bread. This gives them trust and confidence in the world.

Begin with washing hands and then proceed in much the same way as with the younger children, letting them watch. Then, invite them to do a bit of the stirring, pouring in of the various ingredients, and kneading. It is so important that your movements are relaxed and rhythmic for these are what the children will imitate. They can handle larger balls of dough and benefit from the strenuous activity of kneading.

Stories and songs are so helpful at this age and can be used at any phase of the bread making, before, during and after. There are plenty of stories and songs to choose from in this book, or you can make them up. The children may want to act out one of the stories and will certainly incorporate parts of them into their play. This is one way that children digest sensory experiences and make them their own.

In the Steiner/Waldorf kindergartens, baking bread is an essential part of the weekly rhythm. The children help prepare their food in an environment that is intentionally structured as a safe, creative and homey atmosphere. The children are not taught about making bread. They simply do it. Education at this age is about doing things for the joy of doing them. This sets the stage for healthy academic learning later.

In a similar fashion, it is ideal to let children see and help adults working in the garden or with plants that are an essential part of the kindergarten. Garden vegetables and herbs can be used in baking bread and other cooking projects. It is so valuable for children to experience purposeful activity in their own environment. This is how they learn that the good work of our hands is essential for living.

Grade school
Activity time – 1 to 2½ hours
With children aged seven and up, baking bread can be a lesson in itself or can be incorporated into other subject lessons. From the age of nine years or so, once the children can read and do basic mathematics, students can follow a recipe from start to finish and bake for others – their class, parents or school.

One Steiner/Waldorf teacher showed her class how to bake a few times until they were confident in all the steps of the process. She then divided her class into groups of four students, giving each group in turn responsibility for baking bread by the end of each week. The four students busily worked away making challah (recipe on page 90) in the classroom without disturbing the rest of the class, who were engaged in their own work. The teacher just had to make sure everything was ready so that the students could do the rest on their own. When the week's work was done, they broke bread together before saying goodbye.

Of course it is not that easy for all teachers, but it can be so rewarding to bring baking bread into your curriculum. Here are a few ideas for other subjects that can be supplemented with bread activities:

Mathematics
- measuring
- proportions
- fractions
- decimals

Reading
- learning alphabet
- using recipes
- writing recipes
- descriptive essays
- creative writing

History
- international trade
- food and conflict

Cultural studies
- breads around the world
- dietary habits of other cultures

Science
- biology
- chemistry
- nutritional science and health

Art
- sculpture
- recipe creation and innovation

Baking bread will awaken and delight the children and balance out a lesson that might be too dry or heady. It will especially appeal to the kinesthetic learners in the class, who learn best by doing. In the Steiner/Waldorf schools this is an essential part of the curriculum especially in Class 3 (nine-year-olds) in which the practical skills of gardening, cooking and building are emphasised. I have enjoyed building many bread ovens with children of this age. They are so eager to create something imaginative and useful.

Upper school
Activity time – 1 to 3 hours as homework
While upper school or high school teachers are generally strapped for time covering academic subjects, we shouldn't neglect to prepare students for independent living. There are a host of skills that they may or may not have learned. Students getting ready to face the adult world can benefit more than ever from engaging in meaningful work that serves others. Cooking for their peers, for example, is one such rewarding challenge.

There may also be an occasion where some theme could be leavened with a bit of fresh bread. Give them the opportunity and see what emerges. Baking bread could be a part of chemistry, biology, nutrition, history or geography lessons.

Chapter Nine

Seven grains and nutrition

Wheat, rye, rice, barley, millet, oats and maize (corn) are the seven major grains or cereals eaten around the world. Staple foods of most of the world's populations, these grains are energy-rich and packed with nutrition.

Although called grains, the part of the grain that we eat is actually the seed. The plant stores up all its energy (and wisdom) in the seed so it can create the next generation. Seeds are pure potential, like children, waiting to give their gifts to the world.

All about grasses

The seven grains belong to the grass family, which is extensive (over 4000 types) and infinitely helpful to humans. Grasses feed us, provide fodder for our livestock and are used for thatching, building, and for making paper, textiles, starch, oil and sugar. And of course, they carpet our lawns and gardens.

These generous plants usually grow straight up with few leaves or side branching. They stretch towards the sun faster than many plants around them. All grasses are wind pollinated. They expend little energy making beautiful or fragrant flowers. Instead

most flowers are almost invisible showing neither colour nor scent. Their roots generally form shallow mats that stay near the surface of the soil. They are not deep diggers or showy plants. Instead, grasses put all of their effort into forming seeds. It is as if grasses sacrifice flowers, scent, colour, branching and deep roots for their numerous and substantial seeds, which are rich in energy, complex proteins, oils and other nutrients. Most plants produce far more seeds than they actually need to secure their future propagation. They make a surplus that feeds hungry animals and people too. The cereal grains that belong to the grass family are truly our allies, helping sustain life around the globe.

Grains were the first plants which humans grew for sustenance, about 10,000 years ago. Growing and breeding grain originated in the 'Fertile Crescent', in what is now Iraq, and then spread far and wide. To this day no-one knows how our ancestors managed to domesticate grasses. Even with advanced plant technologies, we lack the same ability to be creative with living nature. The grass family and grains remind us of the wisdom human beings once possessed.

A friend of mine, a kindergarten teacher, felt it was important to use all the seven grains in her baking with the children.

Through the process of baking bread each week, the children's imaginations deepened, connecting the seven grains with the forces of nature and to the mystery of human nutrition. She spoke the following poem (see below) with her young students before baking bread together.

Verse for bread making
The sun helps us to grow and lights up our hearts.
The wheat helps us to stand straight.
The rice helps us to grow.
The millet helps us to move.
The rye helps us to be strong.
The oats help us to keep warm.
The barley helps us to persevere.
The corn helps us to dance in the light of the sun.

Erika Grantham

Grains and nutrition

Many nutritionists recommend eating a diet rich in whole grains, vegetables and fresh fruit with a minimum of salt, fat, sugar and processed foods. In so many ways this makes sense. Along with fresh vegetables and fruits, a variety of grains offer balanced nutrition, a variety of flavours and textures. Grains are rich in vitamins, minerals, protein, slow release carbohydrates and all the fibre that is needed for healthy digestion. They release their energy gradually and unlike sugar are sustaining over the long haul.

A variety of fresh vegetables, fruits and whole grains can play a central role, especially for growing children who need plenty of energy, in giving them a balanced diet. This can then be complimented with beans, nuts and smaller amounts of dairy and/or meat as suits each individual. No one diet is suitable for all people and we each have our own particular likes and needs. Eating should be healthy but nonetheless fun, for joy itself is deeply nurturing.

Many UK school cooks are now incorporating whole grains into their menu plans to improve the nutritional value of school meals. Parents and teachers have been quick to comment on how much more focused and attentive well-nourished students are. They are better able to learn and generally more pleasant to be with.

A variety of grains can feature in a rhythmic weekly rotation, accompanied by other fresh produce. In Steiner/Waldorf schools and kindergartens, where I have worked for many years, the prepared lunches are based around the seven grains. Each day of the week is associated with one of them. Various teachers have worked out rotations, connecting the different grains with a day of the week and the seven classical planets, for which the days are named. Here is one suggested rhythm of how to cook with the seven grains:

One need not adhere rigidly to such a scheme, but it forms the basis for creating a varied and healthy diet. Having 'grain days' creates the predictability that children crave. Knowing what to expect gives a child confidence, which in turn will contribute to their ability to be flexible. It has always amazed me how the children look forward to a particular day of the week, especially to Bread day. Even the children that show little interest in foods such as millet at home somehow take to it, when it's offered as part of the kindergarten rhythm.

This approach to serving grains is unusual. No culture I know of commonly eats all seven, because they cannot all be grown in the same climate or ecosystem. Nevertheless, I have found that living with a grain rotation, as I have done for many years, helps me to connect with different cultures, and has provided me (a vegetarian for more than 20 years) with a nutritious and varied diet. Let's take a look at the qualities of each of these seven grains and some of the recipes that might be popular with children.

Grain	Day	Planet
Wheat	Sunday	Sun
Rice	Monday	Moon
Barley	Tuesday	Mars
Millet	Wednesday	Mercury
Rye	Thursday	Jupiter
Oats	Friday	Venus
Maize (corn)	Saturday	Saturn

Wheat
Triticum aestivum

Wheat grows straight and strong, reaching up towards the sun. Its grains are tightly held in a golden seed head. Of all the grains wheat has the most protein, called gluten, and that is why it bakes beautifully into loaves of light and airy bread.

Wheat is the oldest and, currently, the most popular grain in the western world. I discuss the impact of modern wheat on our diet in the next chapter. It is planted in huge fields across Europe and North America throughout their temperate zones and can survive hard winter frosts. These wheat-growing zones are called the bread baskets, or bread belts, of the world. Because of the tremendous size of modern farm fields (with some larger than 4,000 hectares), wheat is harvested by the largest of all farm machines, the combine harvester, that stands as tall as a house.

There are many different varieties of wheat grown today.

Hard Red Spring is a hard, red-brown, high protein wheat used primarily for bread as well as strong flour, bread flour and high gluten flours.

Hard Red Winter is a hard, red-brown, high protein wheat used for bread and hard baked goods. It can be mixed with other flours to increase protein in pastry flour. Some brands of unbleached all-purpose flours are commonly made from hard red winter wheat alone.

Soft Red Winter is a soft, low protein wheat used for cakes, pie crusts, biscuits, and muffins.

Plain flour or cake flour, for example, is made from soft red winter wheat.

Hard White is a hard, light-coloured, opaque, chalky, medium protein wheat planted in dry, temperate areas. It is used for baking bread and brewing beer.

Soft White is soft, light coloured, and very low in protein. It is grown in moist temperate areas and is commonly used for pie crusts and pastry. Plain flour or pastry flour, for example, can be made from soft white winter wheat.

Hard wheats are higher in protein (gluten) and are more difficult to process into flour. Red wheats are usually bleached for cosmetic reasons. Therefore, soft and white wheats generally command higher prices than hard and red wheats on the commodities market.

Other varieties of wheat

Spelt is a more ancient cousin of wheat that is, for many people, easier than wheat to digest. It has a stronger flavour and reacts more quickly with yeast than does wheat. Spelt requires only two thirds of the time to rise but does not have as much protein as strong wheat and thus makes more crumbly breads.

Kamut is a newer variety of wheat grown in the Middle East that may also be suitable for some people who are having difficulty digesting wheat. Kamut, however, is high in the protein gluten and is not suitable for people with coeliac disease. As bread it behaves like a very strong bread flour.

Durum wheat is a very hard wheat used to make semolina flour and pasta. It has a high gluten content and can also be used for baking breads. Durum, like kamut, can be used in breads to make the crumb even chewier.

Emmer wheat and **einkorn** are both early wheat cultivars that are still cultivated in isolated areas today. Use either of these if you can find them, to make authentic, historical breads. Emmer wheat is a very hard wheat and is closely related to durum.

Triticale is a cross-hybridisation between wheat and rye developed in the late 1800s. It grows well on poorer soils and can be used to bake bread or make breakfast cereals. Triticale is high in protein, most of which is not gluten. Try adding up to 25 percent to any wheat recipe.

Menu suggestions
Wholemeal breads
(e.g. page 47), pasta,
pancakes, dumplings
or muffins.

Rice
Oryza sativa

Eat rice before a battle and you will be victorious.

Japanese proverb

Rice is the dietary staple of more than half the world's population. First cultivated in Asia, it is now grown in African and the American continents. Rice could not be more different from wheat. It requires plenty of warmth and moisture and even to be submerged in water for a time. However, it can be grown nearly everywhere, even on steep hillsides, making it a very flexible crop.

Rice is raised in paddies, small fields that can be flooded with water. These can be seen throughout Asia, terraced steps carved into hills and on mountainsides, making efficient use of any available land. Each rice plant is first raised in a nursery and then transplanted by hand into the flooded paddies. Labourers climb the steep hillsides, carrying heavy baskets on their backs and heads. When the rice grains are ripe they droop down towards the water. Then it is time to drain the paddies. Each stalk of rice needs to be cut and gathered together by hand. It is the most labour intensive of all the grains to grow and yet also feeds the greatest proportion of the world's population.

White rice has had its outer husk polished off. It not only loses its brown colour and fibre but also many of its B vitamins, which are essential for the healthy digestion of the starches in rice. This is one of the main causes of malnourishment in Asia today.

There are huge number of varieties of rice that have been developed in different countries including:
- short grain
- long grain
- basmati
- black rice
- Bhutanese red rice
- arborio
- sticky rice

All of these are rich in starches and free of gluten.

Menu suggestions
Rosemary, rice and rye bread (page 62), almond rice muffins (page 108), steamed brown rice and vegetables, hand rolled vegetable sushi, mochi or fried rice.

Barley
Hordeum vulgare

Barley is the humblest of the grains. It can grow in places that are too cold and harsh for either wheat or rye. Barley does not grow very tall and has long spikes, called awns, which emerge from the end of each grain. Because this can look like a beard, it is sometimes called 'old man barley'. It has a short growing season and can be harvested long before the other grains, while the summer sun is still high in the sky.

Barley was once the most important cereal grain in ancient civilisations throughout the Middle East, and was used to make both bread and beer. Barley is now commonly grown for the brewing of beer and whiskey, for which it must first be malted. This is a process in which the grains are soaked in water, left to sprout then gently roasted. Malting makes the grain more digestible and brings out its natural sweetness. Barley malt is a natural sweetener used as a substitute for sugar.

Demeter, the Greek goddess of fertility, is also called the barley mother. This shows how central barley cultivation was to the ancient Greeks, how it can be both the mother and the old man with a beard (see also *Persephone and Demeter*, page 34). During Roman times, the goddess was known as Ceres, from whom we get the word cereal.

Barley was revered as the sustainer of life. The Romans baked it into coarse bread for the common people and for soldiers on the march.

Menu suggestions
Roman army bread (page 66), barley vegetable soup, or steamed like rice with vegetables.

Millet
Pennisetum glaucum, Setaria italica,
Panicum miliaceum and others

Millet is a staple food in many parts of China, Africa and India. It is called the desert grain, because its small grains will grow on even the poorest and driest soils. It can withstand droughts that would kill other grains. Its bushy seed heads come in a vast variety of forms, some as bushy as a fox's tail and others like many fingers. Millet is associated with the fleet footed and ever-changeable god, Mercury. In the west, millet is better known as food for birds, which also embody a similar quality of lightness and quickness of movement. 'A meal of millet,' it is said, 'rests very lightly in your stomach.'

Millet varieties include: pearl millet, foxtail millet, broomcorn millet, teff and sorghum. None of these are related directly to wheat and are easily tolerated by people with coeliac disease as they are free of gluten.

Menu suggestions
Millet poppy birdseed bread (page 64), steamed millet with vegetables or sweet millet with stewed apples.

Rye
Secale cereale

Rye is the newest of all the grains and perhaps the one most closely related to wild grasses. It was not extensively grown until the ancient Romans tamed this 'weed' and cultivated it as a cereal crop.

By the Middle Ages, rye was the favoured grain throughout all Europe, and baked into dark, dense loaves. The wonderful advantage of rye bread is that it can last for weeks without going mouldy. Traditionally villagers would fire their large community bread oven (like the one discussed on page 117) once a month. This was sufficient, as each family could bake enough bread to last a month without it spoiling.

The popularity of rye was overtaken by that of wheat only as recently as the 20th century. However, whole grained, naturally leavened rye loaves remain popular throughout Russia, Germany and Scandinavia.

Rye grows well in harsh northern conditions, where cold, rain and storms are prevalent. It contains some gluten but not enough to make it rise as easily as wheat bread. It is very sustaining, with a strong and distinctive flavour. Experience has shown that it can be difficult to introduce rye bread to children whose palettes are not accustomed to eating it. Many bakers have found success in gradually adding it to wheat breads and thus building a taste for it.

Menu suggestions
Old World rye (page 116), country hearth loaves (page 112) or rye porridge.

Oats
Avena sativa

Oats are the most warming of all the grains with a fat content almost double that of the others. There is a common saying, 'Sowing one's wild oats' that expresses the fiery lustiness that is associated with this energetic grain. Oats can help balance and strengthen the heart and the entire circulatory system. They are also known to help balance cholesterol levels.

Ancient Greeks and Romans considered oats to be animal feed and the Romans were surprised when they encountered the popularity of oats as human food on the British Isles. Oats are easily digested by young and old alike and are usually eaten as porridge. They make a good addition to home-baked bread, cake and biscuits.

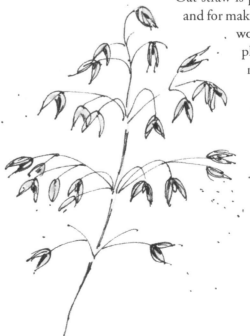

Oat straw is prized for animal bedding and for making corn-dollies, which are woven together from many plants into geometric and representational forms.

Menu suggestions
oatmeal apple raisin bread (page 60), porridge with cinnamon and raisins, granola, muesli or oatmeal cookies.

Maize/corn
Zea mays

Maize or corn is by far the largest and tallest of the grains. Each plant can grow taller than a person, some up to 7 metres (23 feet) high.

According to archaeologists, wild maize was domesticated about 6000 years ago in the Americas. Critical to people's survival, the Aztecs worshipped it, celebrating the plant's different life stages with festivals and offerings. Maize spread to Europe and the rest of the world in the wake of the European

explorers and conquistadors of the late 1500s. Maize continues to be part of nearly every meal in Mexico and other Central American countries.

There is some debate about maize's wild ancestors because maize, as we know it, can only be grown with the aid of human labour. It cannot naturally propagate by itself and would have died out without human intervention. The seed kernels are so tightly bound onto the cob by the many layers of husk that the seeds cannot free themselves to reach the soil to grow. It is only with human assistance that the kernels can be removed from the husk and then be planted in the ground so that maize plants continue to flourish today.

Maize requires plenty of sunshine and a rich fertile soil. It is a heavy feeder, requiring a high level of nitrogen in the soil. Instead of growing its seeds at the top of the plant, as do the other grains, maize forms ears of corn lower down out of the nodes of its lower leaves, hidden away from the sun. Like all grasses, it is wind pollinated. The male flowers, or pollen tassels, rest atop the stalk and rain their yellow pollen over the field of corn. Lower down on the plants, female flowers, or cobs, are forming with corn silk stretching out from what will become the corn kernels. Each potential kernel has its own silken thread to catch a grain of pollen.

Most maize now grown is used to feed cattle. Some sweetcorn is grown for eating fresh.

Other varieties are grown just for tortillas or for popping. Maize has been bred into a whole host of varieties, sizes and colours including yellow, white, red and blue. Maize kernels are rich in oil and starches that are easily converted into sugars. These are often pressed into corn oil and/or made into corn syrup, a commonly used sweetener. Maize is also being converted into ethanol, which can be mixed with gasoline to run cars. Corn mother truly is taking care of her children (also see Grandmother Maize, page 17).

Menu suggestions
corn bread (page 100), fresh corn on the cob, polenta, corn tortillas, corn chowder or popcorn.

Genetically modified (GM) maize
Maize is one of the four main GM crops grown globally on a large commercial scale (the others are soya, rice and oilseed rape).

Other GM products under development include rice, soy beans, oilseed rape (canola), tomato and sweet potato. GM maize accounts for about 30 percent of the GM grown in North America, which grows three-quarters of the world's GM crops. The main GM- growing countries (US, Canada, Argentina and Brazil) do not separate GM ingredients from their non-GM counterparts. According to the UK government's Food Standards Agency, many processed foods in the UK, such as biscuits, cooking sauces, and food coatings, will include GM ingredients at a very low level if they use maize (and soya) as an ingredient. Most GM maize enters the UK as GM feed for non-organic farm animals.

Farmers report that cattle, if given the choice of GM or traditional feed, invariably choose the traditional feed. Organic and biodynamic standards prohibit any type of GM ingredient in any other stage of food production, including GM crops in animal feed.

Chapter Ten

Factory-made bread – wheat sensitivities, allergies and coeliac disease

Sensitivity to wheat and wheat products is a serious health issue. For some people, an intolerance to gluten is lifelong because of a genetic disorder called coeliac disease, discussed in more detail at the end of this chapter. For others, the reasons why wheat causes bloating, indigestion and fatigue are less clear-cut. Having researched bread, and having baked in a variety of contexts, I see that complex factors are involved, and I have come to believe that industrially-produced bread may be detrimental for many peoples' health.

To help you make informed dietary choices, let's take a look at how factory bread is manufactured. Hearing what really goes into most shop-bought bread may inspire you to bake more at home. That way you know what goes into your bread and can guarantee a healthy product.

Refined wheat

Although wheat has been the west's staple, dominant grain for centuries, our consumption – particularly of refined white wheat – has never been greater. Wheat is in nearly everything we eat, not only in bread, pasta, cereals and biscuits, but also in the thickening agents in sauces and ketchups, and in a great many ready-to-eat and processed food products too. Perhaps this huge intake of refined wheat is stretching our body's capacity to digest it. Rather than receiving it as nutrition, the body is treating wheat as an allergen and fighting against it. This might explain the complex wheat intolerance symptoms that some people are experiencing.

How wheat has changed

The wheat we eat today is completely different from the one our parents and grandparents were raised on.

The 20th century method of hybridisation has transformed traditional varieties into new strains of wheat in a relatively short time. These hybrids were bred shorter for easier machine harvesting, with higher protein content so that bread dough increased its machinability, and for greater resistance to fungus and pests. Little emphasis has been placed on developing wheat's nutritional content or on people's ability to digest the final product. The vitamin and mineral content of wheat has dropped dramatically while the protein gluten has grown. Other major impacts on the nutrition and quality of bread come from factory methods of farming, baking and processing.

Wheat was originally bred from naturally occurring grasses, at a crucial point in ancient history when human beings ceased to be nomadic hunter-gatherers and started cultivating the land and storing its harvest. Over the next 10,000 years, farmers saved the best seeds, which they planted the following year. The quality of wheat steadily improved. The seed heads grew larger and the plants more resilient to challenges in the local climate. In traditional agriculture, wheat is often grown as small fields where other crops and abundant wildlife also thrive.

This has all changed. Wheat is mostly cultivated in vast fields that sometimes stretch further than the eye can see. In North Dakota in the Midwest of North America, dubbed the bread basket of the world, some fields cover an area greater than 10,000 acres (5,000 hectares). Only one crop is grown, and only one variety of that crop – hence the term monoculture. Any other plant that tries to grow is systematically poisoned and eliminated. These fields require high inputs of synthetic fertilisers, pesticides and herbicides, none of which are particularly healthy for the land, the farmer or, ultimately, for us as consumers of bread. Pesticide residues are regularly found in government tests of food and their health effects are not yet fully understood.

More protein

Wheat, now a cash commodity crop, has hugely increased in its volume of production. Alongside this, the protein (or gluten) content in the wheat has also grown. One might wonder what is wrong with this. Are not more wheat, and more protein in wheat, achievements to be celebrated? Sadly, high wheat yields have had little impact on world hunger, which is more of an issue of poverty and political will. Most of the malnourished children in the developing world live in countries with food surpluses. In fact, the industrialisation of farming has done much to deprive traditional farmers of their ability to feed their own families.

Factory bread may be produced on a huge scale but it fails to meet our nutritional needs. A host of health problems can ensue with the increased wheat protein in our diets. Gluten tends to cause allergic reactions in many people and now our bodies have to deal with digesting more of it and in higher amounts than ever.

Perhaps this concentration and type of protein is not well suited to the human digestive tract. Our bodies are simply not equipped to deal with modern bread and are showing serious signs of not adjusting very well to this newly created foodstuff.

Seed choice

Farmers typically select the grain they are going to plant based on its growing and harvesting properties. Little information is available to them about its nutrient contents or digestibility. They know that most industrial buyers care only about protein content and so this is what they focus on.

Refined white flour

Not only does each individual grain now contain more gluten and fewer essential minerals, but also the process of turning whole grain into white flour removes valuable nutrients. Modern roller mills mechanically grind then separate the components of the wheat. The heat of the milling process degrades what nutrients are left.

The nutritious inner germ is sifted out as well as the seed's outer coat, the bran, which is the natural fibre that helps us to digest wheat. Brown flour

becomes white and gets a longer shelf life, as there are no fats or oils from the wheat germ to go rancid. Progress has a price: the integrity of wheat has been sacrificed for convenience. Furthermore, many white flours are chemically bleached to make them appear even whiter.

Bread manufacturers may add vitamins and minerals to 'enrich' flours. But research shows that these often-synthetic supplements are not as readily absorbed by the human digestive tract as vitamins and minerals in their natural form. Our bodies know the difference and are not easily fooled.

Additives and enzymes

In the 1960s, industry scientists developed the Chorleywood Bread Process to improve Britain's food security by making bread from domestic wheat despite its traditional low- protein content. In the process they learned how to make loaves of bread in a fraction of the time it had taken in the past. Bread dough is beaten at high speeds in mechanical mixers so that air and water is quickly incorporated into the dough. This beating process requires doubled quantities of quick acting yeast, hydrogenated fats and chemical oxidants in order to dramatically shorten the rising time of the bread to just five minutes. The bread is literally whipped up instead of allowed to rise. The vast majority of bread is now made this way.

Bread factories may be cost efficient, but the spongy white product they produce is nothing like the bread that you or I could bake at home. It is without substance. You can squish an entire loaf into a small pasty ball that has little taste and nutritional value and it is much more difficult to digest.

In Andrew Whitley's book *Bread Matters*, he lists all the ingredients, apart from traditional flour, water, yeast and salt, that go into making a modern loaf of sliced white bread. It makes for uneasy reading, especially knowing that some of the chemicals added do not even appear on the packet's ingredients list. Classified as 'processing aids', non-nutritive enzymes are not required by law to be listed.

Added to the dough to aid manufacture, these enzymes can include alpha-amylase, which is known to cause allergic reactions, and if inhaled by bakers, can trigger asthma. Another enzyme commonly used in factory bread is transglutaminase, which may make wheat protein toxic for those people already sensitive to gluten.

These enzymes, and there are more than a dozen currently in use, are derived from fungal, genetically modified bacteria and animal sources (phospholipase may be derived from the pancreas of pigs and is thus forbidden from kosher and halal diets). Despite being potentially harmful, allergenic and religiously offensive, consumers have no way of knowing how to avoid them.

Less speed, more taste

The traditional process of dough fermentation, that employs yeast or sourdough, allows the natural flavours of wheat to emerge in their own time. The dough gradually ripens as both the yeast and lactobacillus bacteria together digest and break down the wheat. The flavours mature and the nutrients in the wheat become more available for human digestion. In contrast, the Chorleywood process takes less than an hour from start to finish. Technicians may compensate with artificial additives to improve the bread's flavour but there is no contest. Bread's natural flavour has fallen victim to high-speed production.

Bread that is 'fresh baked' in supermarkets is no better. In-store bakeries generally use either a ready-made mix or bake their bread from frozen dough made with the above process. Additives and dough conditioners are then used to make the bread taste and feel 'freshly baked'. I would not recommend it.

How is factory bread stored?

The coup de grâce is delivered by the spraying of a chemical fungicide on factory-produced bread before it is sliced and wrapped in plastic. The fungicide is what allows it to stay 'fresh' on the grocer's shelf for up to seven days. If a fungicide can stop natural mould from forming, it must also require something different from our bodies to digest it. Our digestive tracts are not designed for fungicides and have to go to extraordinary efforts to break down these unnatural substances.

Factory bread places excessive strain on our digestive system as it tries to extract nutrition from a food that is less and less like the one we have been used to eating over the centuries. The white bread of today is truly a completely new food source of highly questionable nutrititional value.

GM wheat

Genetic modification (GM) is a food technology that inserts the gene from one living thing into the DNA of another, often using bacterial hosts because they can penetrate other cells walls. A few years back an attempt to grow GM wheat commercially was averted largely thanks to the concerted efforts of Canadian farmers. The public's rejection of GM in Europe has ensured that it has kept GM food at bay, at least for now.

Organic and biodynamic standards ban GM ingredients from every stage of food production.

Reasons for difficulty in digesting factory bread:

- high proportion of wheat in our diets
- hybridised wheat with high protein
- monoculture
- artificial fertilisers
- pesticides
- herbicides
- fungicides
- monoculture baking yeast
- refining and chemically bleaching flour
- additives, dough conditioners and enzymes
- preservatives
- lack of joy in the manufacture
- any combination of the above

While scientists and nutritionists are still debating the evidence, it makes common sense to avoid the health risks associated with highly processed bread. From a holistic perspective, such bread is no longer the staff of life. In fact, it may well be contributing to our declining health.

Sensitive or allergic to wheat?

By far the simplest solution is to reduce or eliminate the amount of wheat that you are consuming. But, as we have seen, it may not be the wheat itself that is the problem but one of the many 'innovations' used in its manufacture. These can be dealt with by making sure that any wheat you eat is organic or biodynamic, and whole grained. Whole grains (that includes the seed's husk, or bran) contain all that you need for effective digestion. Organic or biodynamic farming ensures that potentially harmful farm chemicals such as synthetic fertilisers, herbicides, pesticides and fungicides are avoided.

Organic and biodynamic approaches also prohibit processing aids with known health risks, including enzymes made from genetically modified or animal sources.

Sourdough breads for easy digestion

I have found that many people can more easily digest sourdough breads. The natural sourdough leaven initiates some of the body's work of digesting the wheat. It breaks down starches, and proteins including gliadin and gluten to which many people seem most sensitive. It also makes the nutrients in the wheat more bio-available by breaking down the phytic acid in the wheat bran that otherwise limits the uptake of these essential minerals.

Furthermore, it might be that some people have become sensitive to quick-rising yeasts that are manufactured from a highly refined single variety of yeast. Made by fermenting flour with water, sourdough's natural leaven is a complex community of yeasts and lactobacillus bacteria that more completely break down the components of the grain. In addition you have the reassurance that sourdough's natural leavening process has been used by cooks for centuries.

A recent study in Italy demonstrated that sourdough leaven was so successful in breaking down harmful gluten and gliadin proteins that a majority of research subjects who were highly allergic to wheat protein were able to eat sourdough bread with no gastric distress.

Wheat intolerance: substituting with other grains

I have included some wheat-free recipes. Otherwise, you can usually replace wheat with other grains in your favourite recipes. Many people who are wheat-sensitive find that they can tolerate (indeed, enjoy) low-gluten grains such as rye, or spelt, a more ancient cousin of our modern wheat. See which grains work best for you. You may have to experiment because how food affects your body is an individual affair. There are of course other grains that have no gluten whatsoever (listed below in the section on coeliac disease) that can act as substitutes.

A wheat-free period

You might well have to give up wheat for a time to allow your system to re-equilibrate. Once your body has cleansed itself of toxins, you may then be able to tolerate small amounts of wheat again. Please consult your physician if you are considering drastic changes to your diet.

Coeliac disease

First diagnosed in the 1950s, coeliac disease (coeliac sprue or total gluten intolerance) can be a genetic disorder and a lifetime condition. In coeliac disease, gluten causes the immune system to produce antibodies that attack the delicate lining of the bowel, which is responsible for absorbing nutrients from food. Symptoms can be subtle, and people may feel unwell for some time before a diagnosis is made. Symptoms include diarrhoea, nausea, weight loss, and malnutrition. It mostly affects people of European (especially Northern European) descent, and now affects nearly 1 in 150 people in North America. Recent studies show that it also can affect

Hispanic, Black and Asian populations as well. Those affected suffer damage to the villi in their intestines when they eat gluten found in wheat, rye, barley and frequently oats.

Oats don't contain gluten but a gluten-like protein which some people may react to. Oat products may be contaminated by wheat, rye or barley during processing.

The only effective treatment at the moment is a restrictive diet that is completely free of any form of gluten.

Doves Farm, Red Mill, Glutafin, Orgran and many other manufacturers make gluten-free baking mixes. Many of these have recipes included on the package. The ingredients are usually made from a variety of grain, potato and bean starches combined with gelatin and xantham gum.

For more information on wheat sensitivities, allergies and coeliac disease please consult your physician and refer to the books and websites listed in the bibliography.

The following grains are generally considered to be safe for people with coeliac disease to eat:
- corn
- rice
- amaranth
- buckwheat (or kasha)
- chickpeas (garbanzos)
- Job's tears (Hato Mugi, Juno's Tears, River Grain)
- lentils
- millet
- peas
- quinoa
- ragi
- sorghum
- soy
- tapioca
- teff
- wild rice

Chapter Eleven

Author's bread biography

Growing up in 1960s suburban America, I ate the standard commercial bread that came in plastic bags. We stored it in the freezer to keep it from spoiling. The white sliced bread could be kept frozen for nearly a year before getting freezer burn. It tasted terrible.

While my childhood featured lovingly prepared, home-cooked meals, bread, like all carbohydrates, was considered fattening and was relegated to sandwiches for school lunches, functional kid's food.

Bread held that which was placed between it from getting all over your hands and filled us up too. My sisters and I ate sandwiches every day for lunch: peanut butter, peanut butter and jelly, peanut butter and cheese, peanut butter and... Our inventiveness knew no bounds. As to the quality of this bread, we gave it little thought. The spongy white centre was more desirable than the tan crust, but growing children ate all. We baked cakes and pies, but never bread. That joy was yet to come.

It was not until I was 20 that I baked my first loaf. My motivation came not from wanting to produce healthy or even edible bread, but to fulfil a sculptural inspiration. I wanted to create life-sized, human sculptures that would biodegrade with the help of animals and the weather. And the choice of materials soon narrowed to using hand-baked loaves of bread, invisibly joined together with wooden skewers. I wanted to create environmental sculptures that I could place in natural settings, then watch and record their gradual decay at the mercy of the elements. In the end there was nothing left but photographs and memories of this creative and destructive process.

So, with absolutely no baking experience, I dove into huge sacks of flour. I learnt by trial and error (make that errors), baking huge amounts without a recipe. After several disasters, I developed a feel for the dough. If it was too sticky to work with, I added more flour.

If it was too dry to knead, I added more water. And with active yeast, the rising simply happened, if I was patient enough. My method more or less worked but was not reliable and tasted terrible. Nevertheless, it performed well as a sculptural medium and I built each of these 'BREADMAN' installations in just a few days. These life-sized sculptures were made from sometimes dense, sometimes pallid, white bread. It was not until my second bread sculpture, when I had other contributing artists to sustain, that I became interested in baking good tasting bread as well.

One bread sculpture I created was entitled 'Lovers devoured at a picnic'. It comprised a woman and man reclining on the lawn of the Woodmere Art Museum in Philadelphia, USA. Between them was a picnic basket made of bread, filled with bread renditions of fruit and cheese and other picnic favourites. Every part of the couple was made of bread, even their hats.

The bread figures reclined on the lawn for nearly three months, delighting many visitors. Some school groups visited more than once to watch the process of construction and decomposition. A few children visited every day and joined the bread couple at their picnic. Besides that, the local squirrels and crows took regular nourishment from the sculpture.

Gradually the man and woman dispersed into two graceful arcs of crumbs across the museum lawns. The three-dimensional sculpture transformed into a two-dimensional painting of white specks on green. And then, crumb-by-crumb, they disappeared altogether. This sculpture and others in the series were entertaining and provocative experiences that led me to build more bread sculptures in collaboration with dozens of artists across North America.

Bread art soon found its way into other parts of life. I began teaching children in a small home-schooling community in Oregon, USA, called Lost Valley Educational Center. We baked regularly. We sang. We played. We told each other stories and acted them out during or in between the bread-making process. We fitted our lessons around the natural rhythms of the bread dough, attuning ourselves to its needs, learning what it had to teach us about purposeful work, rhythm and patience, mathematics and cultural history too.

We kneaded our joy, our laughter, our songs and our prayers right into the loaves. People could taste these in the substance of the bread. The joy we had in baking bread was contagious for all that ate it.

These experiences built a tangible sense of confidence that we (teacher and children) could make a valuable contribution to the quality of everyone's lives at the community. Even a five-year-old child could make bread that was worthy of being served to guests, giving both nourishment and pleasure.

Then, as a class teacher at the Olympia Waldorf School, bread baking grew into a significant part of our school curriculum from kindergarten through to grade 8. I taught the same group of children for eight years, from first grade through to eighth. The children and I baked weekly in the early grades.

Sometimes we practised forming our letters and numbers out of bread dough. We made soft pretzels, a host of animals and imaginative creatures and then had the pleasure of eating them as well as sharing them with others. We baked wholesome bread, rolls and loaves and churned our own butter. Bread brought a lightness and joy to our academic work.

In third grade (ages nine and ten) we went through all the stages of the bread-making from seed to table, including building our own earthen oven and bakery shelter to protect it from the elements. At every step, we participated with our hands and hearts.

First, we cleared a small field next to our classroom. Half was for individual student plots and the other half was for wheat. In the autumn we sowed it, broadcasting winter wheat seeds into its waiting soil.

We attended our wheat patch daily through the waning days of autumn and watched as the green shoots broke through the soil. At first they grew quickly but then slowed as winter advanced. They slept through darkest winter, but in the spring the green plants surged again towards the sun, growing to the height of the children's chests. And

the summer sun saw the grains ripen to fullness atop their stalks, the plants turning from green to golden brown.

We harvested the seed by hand with small sickles and scissors. Over the next few months, we threshed our entire harvest with stomping feet, whenever someone had the energy to do so, breaking the grains free from stalk and chaff. On a windy day we winnowed the wheat, pouring it from one basket to another, time and again. The inedible parts of the grain, the chaff, were carried away by the wind, leaving the ripe kernels of wheat clean and ready for grinding. These

were perfect tasks for the children, especially those needing extra physical activity to help them stay focused. It was truly purposeful work.

Next we set out to design and build an earthen bread oven for the school's kindergarten garden. The children sawed, hammered and chiselled wood for a structure to protect it from the rain, then kneaded the mud and straw to build the bread oven itself. Everyone was fully engaged in the process, which was an integral part of our year's studies in farming and house building. The parents joined in too. And it was most interesting and informative to see which children would gravitate to which jobs, especially who wanted to stomp in the mud pit.

At last The Bakery, as we called it, was completed, along with our threshed, winnowed and hand milled wheat. The crowning moment of this year-long process came when we fired up the new oven to bake our first loaves. Inexperience led us to fire the oven too hot. The children so enjoyed feeding the fire and were quite responsible about doing so safely, but it became much hotter than necessary. We put the loaves in anyway and they cooked in only 15

minutes, a bit charred on the outside, but perfect on the inside. Never mind the char, the children ate every last crumb of this hard-won whole wheat bread. What satisfaction! Even now, 10 years later, the children still remember it as the best-tasting bread ever.

That oven and those experiences have led me to build other bread ovens with children in the USA and England. Baking in this old-world way enables children to participate in the entire process. They are creating something from scratch, working with the natural elements to make life-sustaining bread.

I continue to pursue this way of working in my 'Art of Baking Bread' workshops in England, Italy, Canada and further afield. Often, we bake in ovens that I have created with the students. It is a privilege to teach the art of baking bread in these hand-crafted earthen ovens brought to life with wood fires. This process enhances bread-baking immeasurably for all involved and makes the most satisfying loaves.

I should add that I first fell in love with my dear wife, Luciana, while we were baking together for a weekend at Emerson College. The magic of baking bread in an earthen oven awakened in us the magic in one another. We now have two daughters both of whom have a love of good bread and are quite accomplished bakers and bread oven builders. Never could I have imagined that the simple act of baking bread would play such a significant role in my life. I am well blessed by it. I hope that someday you will share the experience and come bake with me.

Appendix I

The benefits of organic and biodynamic food

Why chose organic and biodynamic ingredients?

You can increase bread's healthiness and taste by making it from organic and biodynamic ingredients. These are grown and produced as close to nature as possible. The roots of the growing grains reach deep in soil enriched by natural methods. Milk comes from cows fed, as nature intended, on grass and clover. Eggs are from chickens living in small flocks and free to range. No wonder food from such farms tastes better.

As well as having more of the good things, organic and biodynamic food also excludes more of the bad things. Pesticides are avoided, chemical fertilisers and genetic modification (GM) are banned. There is no place for food additives with health risks or artificial food colourings.

Organic and biodynamic farming is more than farming without chemicals. It's a philosophical approach, combining traditional practices with modern research. The aim is to produce food of the highest quality with the least disturbance to nature. Farmers have to be finely attuned to their land and animals to achieve this. Nature holds the answers to many agricultural problems. Organic and biodynamic farmers aim to tap into this biological fount of knowledge. For instance, they control pests by nurturing wild areas around their fields to encourage a pest's natural predators, and use compost to replenish the soil.

Fertilisers

As they grow, plants absorb nutrients from the soil. These nutrients must be replaced or the soil suffers. Chemical fertilisers add a very limited amount of artificially-made nutrients to the plant that bypass the soil and its subterranean life. In time, chemically-fertilised soil becomes lifeless as its microbes, so essential to soil health, die out.

Organic and biodynamic methods introduce a wide range of nutrients, including trace minerals, by using compost, crop rotations and growing green manures. A cover crop of clover, for instance, builds long-term fertility, naturally fixes nitrogen and increases the activity of soil microbes.

Nourishing the soil with organic matter also helps alleviate climate change. According to the Rodale Institute, the soil's natural capacity for storing carbon is significantly increased with organic and biodynamic methods.

In contrast chemical fertilisers increase greenhouse gases because their manufacture depends entirely on fossil fuels. Factory-made fertiliser is the largest source of carbon dioxide emissions in agriculture.

Everything is connected. Clover builds nitrogen that helps store carbon. Cows love clover, and clover-eating cows produce nutritious milk. Organic and biodynamic farming creates many such virtuous cycles that are elegant, simple and efficient.

More good things
A growing body of scientific research shows that food produced by organic and biodynamic methods has a higher nutritional content than non-organic food.

Here is one example. Organic cows are fed a natural diet, high in grass and clover. As a result their milk contains higher levels of vitamins and antioxidants as well as higher levels of omega-3 essential fatty acids, so vital for our health.

Because organic and biodynamic farmers avoid using pesticides, plants activate their own self-defence mechanisms against pests and disease. These antioxidants both guard the plants and, when we eat them, protect our health.

Avoiding pesticides is also good for wildlife. Organic and biodynamic farms support more butterflies, beetles, birds, bats and wild plants than non-organic farms. The largest UK study so far has found there were twice as many wild plants in organic fields. The researchers said farming without pesticides could help restore the countryside's wildlife.

Birth of the organic and biodynamic movements
The development of bombs in the first world war dramatically changed the face of farming. After the war, chemical companies turned from producing munitions to making farm fertilisers. Crops fertilised with artificially- produced nitrogen grew faster but the soil suffered. Farmers no longer replenished the soil with organic matter, resulting in soil erosion. The loss of recycled nutrients reduced crop quality, impacting on human and animal health.

Different groups emerged in the western world to counteract the damaging effects of industrialisation. Biodynamic agriculture originated thanks to a group of German farmers. Concerned about the degeneration of their soil, they approached the Austrian philosopher, scientist and social reformer, Rudolph Steiner, for advice. Shortly before he died in 1924, he gave a series of lectures on sustainable holistic agriculture, which inspired the international biodynamic movement. In Britain the Biodynamic Agricultural Association's parent group was founded in 1928.

In 1905 the British government sent Sir Albert Howard, an agricultural scientist, to India to assist local farmers with farming. The scientist spent the next 25 years learning from them. Traditional farming showed him simple truths: how composting helped produce high-quality feed so livestock were healthy enough to resist disease, including foot and mouth. Like Steiner, he understood how the health of soil is the basis of plant, animal and human health. His research inspired the international organic movement and led to the founding of the Soil Association in 1946.

Sir Albert Howard and fellow pioneers predicted that food shortages during the second world war – and its need to produce more food with less manpower – would force farms to become more like factories. Indeed, they were right. Mechanisation increased and, following lobbying by the chemical companies, farmers had to use artificial fertilisers.

Despite public support, and vigorous, learned opposition from the new organic movement, organic methods were sidelined and chemical farming came to dominate agriculture.

Slowly people have realised what has been lost. As a result organic and biodynamic farming has grown in popularity. Perhaps it is not surprising that a system which inherently respects the soil, animals and wildlife, and does not treat a farm like a factory, produces delicious and healthy food.

How do I know it's organic and biodynamic?

The term 'organic' on food labels is a legal definition in the European Union. It is the only food system (apart from baby food) inspected and certified under a rigorous annual inspection process. The Soil Association certifies over 70 percent of organic food sold in the UK.

The Biodynamic Agricultural Association (BDAA) certifies to organic and internationally recognised Demeter standards. The latter guarantees that all biodynamic as well as organic practices are being followed.

Organic standards can vary but those of the Soil Association and BDAA are amongst the most rigorous.

Organic and biodynamic – similarities and differences

The definition of sustainability is 'development that meets the needs of the present without compromising the ability of future generations to meet their own needs.' [The Brundtland Commission (Our Common Future), 1987]

Organic and biodynamic farmers are companions on the same fascinating journey. They believe in the interconnectedness of all living things, putting back what they take out and working in harmony with nature.

However there are subtle and important differences between the two farming types and I will attempt a broad description.

Biodynamic agriculture recognises that life on earth has a spiritual context. The farm is a living entity, a microcosm of the greater whole. The biodynamic farmer strives for balance, so if a farm cannot produce enough feed for its farm animals, this is a sign that the balance needs addressing. This consciously spiritual approach ensures that biodynamic farms cannot readily be swallowed up by a mechanistic supermarket culture.

Thanks to Rudolph Steiner's insights, biodynamic farmers use a series of nine preparations to energise the soil and plants and increase their vitality. Made from natural and organic materials such as herbs or dung, small quantities are progressively diluted in rainwater. According to the principles of homeopathy, this increases their potency. In biodynamics, the solution is stirred in a special way for about an hour, creating a swirling vortex, first going one way, then another, energising it further. You can buy these preparations from the BDAA.

The quality of food and its keeping properties are further enhanced by using an astronomical calendar (also available from the BDAA) to achieve the best times for sowing, cultivating and harvesting. As one Indian biodynamic farmer explained, 'The lunar cycle casts a tremendous effect on the size and formation of plant roots and their growth, and farmers can get a good yield if they sow their crops in accordance with the lunar phase. This is an ancient method, which was practised by our forefathers and lost along the way. It has now been accepted and scientifically proved.'

Both organic and biodynamic farmers believe the farm is a 'closed' system. By recycling nutrients, it can constantly renew and replenish itself. Farmers vary in how much organic matter they import from outside their farms but ideally everything they need, from fertilisers to pesticides, is available in their own fields. They ban all artificial fertilisers, herbicides and fungicides and any use of GM.

Both organic and biodynamic standards place enormous value on animal welfare. The farm animals are truly free-range, with plenty of space and easy access to the outdoors. Farm antibiotics are used only when absolutely necessary. Instead farmers build up their animals' immune system through careful husbandry, checking the animal has all it needs to be healthy: good organic nutrition, freedom to express their natural behaviour, while the size of flocks or herds are kept small enough to reduce stress.

Both organic and biodynamic standards also ban any post-harvest chemical treatments with a known health risk. As for processed food, only about 30 of the most innocuous additives are allowed, compared to the 500 or so used without restriction in the non-organic food industry. Organic standards in the UK have always banned harmful additives such as hydrogenated fats, monosodium glutamate and aspartame and all artificial flavourings (30,000 are currently used by the food industry) and all colourings (apart from natural annatto in cheese).

These decisions are based on a founding belief, the precautionary principle: if a significant risk exists, don't take it. Thanks to this attitude, organic and biodynamic standards guard the purity of food.

Safe from GM

Genetic modification (GM) attempts to artificially insert the gene from one living thing into the DNA of another. Once this gene is inserted into a living thing, the latter is said to be genetically modified. Once 'modified', GM companies can patent the process, enabling them to own the GM plant. If this plant cross-pollinates with a farmer's non-GM crop, they own that too, according to a 2003 ruling by the Supreme Court of Canada. This suggests GM is more about increasing profits and food control than feeding the world – despite what the companies claim.

The main GM crops have been created to make industrial farming a smoother operation. For instance GM soya makes weed elimination easier because the crops have been 'modified' to survive being sprayed with a particular herbicide.

In the case of GM maize, it has been programmed to produce an insecticide, normally produced by the bacteria, bacillus thuringiensis (BT). Thus the crop kills its own maize pests, without spraying. However, because the crop never stops producing this toxin, the insects soon get resistant.

The long-term human health implications of these methods are unknown and untested. However there is enough evidence to cause concern. Several animal feeding trials show animals fed GM maize suffer more disease or death than animals fed on non-GM maize. There are also reports of human ill-health in the Philippines associated with proximity to GM maize fields. Despite public opposition in the UK to GM food, GM is coming in through the 'back door' as imported animal feed. Food from GM-fed animals can contain GM materials, according to several studies, including two that found GM maize DNA in cow's milk.

Eating organic and biodynamic food on a budget

You are taking the first step by baking your own bread. One of the biggest expenses is buying processed organic food, such as biscuits or ready-meals, so try if you can cooking from scratch.

People sometimes ask: if I have to choose a few ingredients to be organic, which ones should I opt for? When it comes to bread, it makes sense for the largest quantities, such as flour, to be organic or biodynamic.

Avoid shopping in supermarkets, especially when it comes to seasonal produce and food grown in your own country. Buying seasonally, direct from local farmers (via farm shops, farmers' markets, or a vegetable box delivered to your door) is a more economical way of buying organic or biodynamic produce.

Buying locally also provides the best value for money because this is often the freshest and best-tasting food around. Buying locally also lessens food miles, reduces the bargaining power of supermarket chains, creates more money for your local community (money doubles its value when spent locally) and supports your local farms. Shopping locally also helps you develop a sense of community. Getting to know your farmer creates a connection with your food and how it is grown, which adds to the whole experience.

You can keep costs down even further by forming or joining a buying group. This could be a group of friends, colleagues or neighbours making up a bulk order with a farmer or wholesaler and getting it delivered to one place.

Alternatively you could join (or form) a community agriculture scheme (CSA). Families take part in a farm's activities, helping with hoeing and harvesting, in exchange for a share of the produce. It gives a real sense of involvement, a genuine opportunity to get to know where your food comes from. Instead of steering your children down a supermarket aisle, they could follow a farm trail. Is there a better way to learn about food?

Elisabeth Winkler, former editor of the Soil Association's *Living Earth* magazine

Appendix II

Building a real bread culture: from farm to plate

Why does real bread matter?

Bread is 'a coming home'. Real bread is a coming home to ourselves, our loved ones and our community. In days gone by, villages would bring in the wheat harvest together. Now, by baking bread, we can rekindle some small vestiges of that sentiment.

Breaking bread is also a spiritual belonging, as depicted in the Last Supper. In these times of ever greater distraction, bread can be a way within, to the Inner Light. Bread is a symbol of alchemy, of the bringing together of ingredients to transform them in the womb of the oven into something new. Within this alchemy, we can find transformation in ourselves.

Warren Lee Cohen's book, *Baking Real Bread*, offers timely, practical ways of building the real bread movement, in families, schools and communities. It is about rebuilding 'real bread culture' by baking with children in creative, imaginative ways, not just easy to bake recipes, but with stories, songs and blessings.

How can we rebuild the local, real bread economy?

The Reclaim the Grain movement is about people coming together to localise and reclaim their regional grain economies. It is about enabling farmers, millers, bakers and families to use their own grains in their own supply system. Often this includes heritage grains. Farmers, bakers, millers and communities can work together to decentralise grain processing facilities and bring more diversity to our fields, ideally utilising the heritage varieties which best adapt to your particular soils and climate. The local grain networks in the UK and in North America are collaborating to achieve this.

The power of story can help build the real bread movement, for example by drawing on Warren Lee Cohen's stories. Stories can engage people with a local sense of identity and belonging, linked to the unique crops grown by their local farmers and as a celebration of the artisans making nourishing products from them. Schools can also engage children, for example when Stroud's Tom Herbert, the Real Bread Campaign ambassador and star of

Channel 4 TV's The Fabulous Baker Brothers, visited Horsley School in Gloucestershire to help students sow wheat at the Bake Your Lawn launch. https://www.sustainweb.org/news/jan12_real_bread_byl2012_launch/

What are the benefits of real bread?

On a nutritional basis, real, sourdough bread made from heritage and landrace grains, is one of the most important sources of pre-biotics we can attain to feed our gut flora. Landrace grains are those adapted to particular local land and soil conditions. Real bread is a rich source of micro nutrients and, unlike modern grains, can act in an anti inflammatory way rather than a pro inflammatory way in our bodies. Moreover, when we eat food which has a connection to our own sense of meaning and of place, we feel nourished in more than the physical sense.

Making real bread slows us down. You cannot cheat the sourdough process, it needs time and this slows our pace, offering us a container in which to unwind from mental stress and enjoy the fruits of our work in a very real sense. When we bake we are working with life forces, as the flour, water and salt are transformed through the magical process of the sourdough ferment. It is more and more important today, with the increasing influence of electronic technology, that we engage in processes which are as full of life forces as possible.

What is the story of heritage grains? How was heritage wheat rediscovered by farmers such as John Letts?

The John Letts story I first heard of is that when thatching, he found ancient ears of wheat in the old thatch. However, the seminal moment for John came when he was working at the Oxford Museum of Natural History, analysing the remains of plants found at archaeological sites to draw conclusions

about food diet, grains, farming systems and climate. One day someone brought him a shoe box full of blackened straw taken from a mediaeval house where the original thatch was being stripped to the rafters and replaced:

'I was sitting at Thomas Henry Huxley's old desk in the museum when the lid came off, and there were 20 kinds of wheat in this one box, and every ear was different. This was from the base layer of thatch, which historically was never changed. And this one box of thatch preserved in the smoke of a mediaeval hall was like a time capsule of information about 16th -century farming. So I began to search out and grow old varieties of wheat to provide good quality straw for thatching. I collected wheat from all over the world, from farmers and gene banks, and put them together to breed a hardy, deep rooted landrace that would grow well in a low-nutrient environment and on a range of soils and weather conditions.'

According to Oliver Tickell, John's dream is for biodiverse local landrace cereal varieties for every farmer, which have adapted to their local soils and micro-climates, with the grains either milled on the farms or by local millers, in turn supplying local bakers making unique local breads.

Most peasant bakeries in France now grow evolutionary heritage populations of wheat. Heritage wheat is generally described as being tall straw varieties from before the 1950s or 'The Green Revolution', when modern wheat was bred in earnest.

A very brief history of wheat

Bread wheat, *Triticum Aestivum*, is the result of a number of crossings, originating in a cross between wild goat grass and wild Einkorn. What many people call 'ancient' varieties include Einkorn, Emmer and Spelt. They all have a husk and need to be put through a dehulling machine before being milled. While not being overly expensive, these machines are not easy to come by if you don't have access to one in your area.

Bread wheat varieties are all 'free threshing', which means they can be threshed after harvest with a combine. The French peasant farmer generally decides to grow wheat populations due to their genetic diversity and evolutionary capacity, which is described in more detail later in this section. During the milling process the bran of the free threshing varieties is separated by the sieving process.

In the book *Restoring Heritage Grains*, Eli Rogosa describes learning from findings at the 12,000 year old Temple Gobekli Tepe, located in Turkey:

'Conventional anthropologists thought that the domestication of wheat and civilization was driven by ecological forces such as the warming after the Ice Age. What we are learning in Göbekli Tepe is that civilization is a product of the human psyche itself, the striving for meaning that thereby created agriculture. This is the opposite of what anthropologists conventionally thought.'

This is a very important understanding. The act of cultivating these heritage wheats is a search for meaning, a way to spend one's time producing food which is meaningful to people, and therefore demonstrates value in a way which is more than solely monetary.

What is YQ wheat? What is population wheat and its benefits?

Wakelyn's YQ (Yield/Quality) wheat is a 'composite cross population', created in 2002 by the late Professor Martin Wolfe at Wakelyn's Farm in Suffolk, UK. Twenty distinct wheat varieties – both modern and older – were crossed with each other

and the resulting hybrids were mixed and sown together to form a 'population' with a very high degree of genetic diversity. Many generations later, the YQ population has evolved in various parts of the UK and has been subject to extensive evaluation by scientists at the Organic Research Centre in Berkshire, UK. (Reference: Scotland the Bread: https://scotlandthebread.org)

YQ is not considered to be a 'heritage' population, and from a baking perspective, does not offer the flavour profile of heritage wheat, but is nonetheless a valuable innovation in the context of a transition from uniformity to diversity.

How do breads baked from organically or biodynamically grown wheat differ in quality, texture and taste from conventionally grown wheat? And how does bread baked from freshly milled flour compare? What do bakers prefer?

There are so many different heritage varieties and many different modern varieties too, though general distinctions between the two can be drawn. There is a relationship between the flavour qualities of a variety and the adaptability of the plant. For instance heritage varieties have more extensive root structures and form better associations in the soil with mycorrhizae. The result of this is better disease prevention and better micro nutrient uptake. Biodynamic farms will be supporting much more life in their soils and give a much better opportunity for mycorrhizae to thrive, therefore increasing the likelihood of better flavour and nutrition profiles.

There is another important distinction between modern and heritage varieties. Modern varieties are less able to differentiate between what is good for them and what is a pathogen, due to much of the genetic memory having been bred out of them. So on the one hand they can absorb a lot of nitrogen but they will also be more susceptible to diseases. Due to their poorer root structures, they will be less able to thrive on soils not 'pumped up' on NPK (i.e. nitrogen, potassium, phosphorus fertiliser).

Heritage grains are also softer than modern grains, and this aids digestibility with the gluten structures in heritage varieties differing from modern varieties. When baking, these glutens are more delicate and this requires greater skill from the baker and may not result in the loaf with the same 'rise' and volume as a modern wheat sourdough. In my view, what you gain is superior in terms of character, flavour, and digestibility.

How freshly our flour is milled is very important. As a peasant baker, I use flour milled the day before baking. Freshly milled, stone ground flour contains all of the beneficial enzymes, which oxidise in about three weeks after milling, losing valuable nutritional substance.

Many bakers are less used to working with freshly milled flour and traditionally let the flour age past three weeks so it becomes easier to work with. However, I personally have never had a problem baking with fresh flour.

How can families, communities such as CSAs and schools grow their own wheat and other grains on a small scale, harvest and mill it?

A good resource for this is the 'Bake your Lawn' toolkit, produced by the real bread campaign in the UK, which you can download. It is designed for schools.
https://www.sustainweb.org/realbread/bake_your_lawn/

One acre of heritage wheat will normally yield about a ton of wheat, which equates to about a ton of bread. 4m² of heritage wheat will yield about 1kg of grain, possibly more.

So, why not imagine that as a school, family, or perhaps as a joint project with friends, you could grow an acre or half an acre of your own wheat? There is indeed labour involved, and this can engage community spirit. One interesting aspect is that the hand harvesting of grain, rather than combining, is more able to achieve the best quality of grain as the grains are able to finish ripening and harden in the sheaf. So, when you come to harvest your grain, remember to do so when the last flushes of green are still in the straw, then make a rick in the field or bring them into your barn for ripening off and threshing and winnowing over the winter, as you need the grain.

Threshing the grain by hand is best done in my experience by making a flail, consisting of a long stick, attached by a rope to a shorter stick, which you can swing at the sheaves in the floor and beat the grain from the ear. With two people, this can be quite rhythmical and fun. Be sure to have a sheet underneath to catch the grain and once you have the grain, you can winnow by tipping from one bucket or box into another either on a gusty day, as would have been done in the long barns, channelling the wind, or by using an electric fan to blow the chaff from the wheat as the grain passes between the buckets.

When growing for schools, you will want to do the sowing and harvesting in term time, so you will need to choose between a late sowing of winter wheat, or using spring wheat varieties which is often the preference. Winter wheat can be sown in January if the ground is not frozen, resulting in a harvest in early September when term time resumes.

Spring wheat varieties can be sown until the end of April with a harvest later in September.

Are there any home mills that work? Or is it better to buy freshly milled grains from local millers?

I am an advocate of the Astrie stone mill, made in France. However, in North America, the 'New American stone mills' have become popular. Both of these types of mills are small commercial mills and the expense for one household would be too much. Though I do think that a group of households sharing the purchase and running of a small mill could be an excellent option.

The small 'commercial' stone mills offer better quality of flour than the tabletop mills for home kitchens. The tabletop mills are quite rough in their method, utilising very coarse volcanic stones to pulverise the grains. This means it becomes hard to sift all of the bran from the flour. The Astrie mill gently de-envelopes the grain as it rolls out between the stones which are balanced very precisely using a bearing and springs. If you have a local artisanal mill, that would be ideal, but if you don't, then a small tabletop mill still offers you that opportunity to mill your own grain fresh for relatively little expense.

What are the benefits of buying locally, such as from artisan bakeries?

The word 'companionship' can be understood to mean 'with bread', *'con - pan'*.

The joys in our life are more appreciated when shared with others. Creating a web of local relationships through food production can provide a sound basis for the desired future we are building. Running a small artisanal bakery is both a highly skilled job and one which may be economically risky. Artisan bakers need all the community and customer support they can get! Customers can also be advocates for the use of more heritage grains in their breads.

What is a Peasant Bakery?

The peasant baker is someone who grows, mills and bakes with heritage grains on a small scale, normally producing around 300-600 loaves per week. It is a model which combines tradition and innovation with the aims of producing the best possible quality of bread from nutritionally dense grains while securing the livelihoods of small scale agroecological farmers.

The key elements which make a peasant bakery:
- Heritage varieties of wheat, usually populations (mixtures of varieties)
- Stone milling on the farm
- Wood fired oven
- Handmade dough using a dough trough
- Sourdough fermentation

Due to the development of the combine harvester and small scale electric mills, growing, milling and baking are now able to be carried out by one producer. This is an example of a technology which empowers the farmer and baker, rather than agribusiness. It is also a model which allows the farmer to add value on the farm in the same way in which a shepherd may sell cheese rather than just milk. This gives an opportunity to sustain small-scale, agroecological food production, feed local communities and de-centralise wheat, bread and flour production.

The peasant baking movement has become well established in France and Italy but is less known in other countries. Near Totnes in South Devon, the Apricot Centre at Huxhams Cross Farm partnered with Parsonage Farm and the Almond Thief Bakery to found Dartington Mill. This is an innovative venture that sees two farmers, a miller and a baker come together to grow organic and biodynamic specialist wheats, grains and pulses, process these locally and then bake them into delicious bread and sell the products to their fabulous local community. This keeps their food system local, nutritious and sustainable, crucial for mitigating climate change.

Rupert's story with bread

I will never forget my mentor Nicolas Supiot's answer when I asked him in his bakery, 'From whom did you learn?' 'The flour,' was his reply.

Coming from a small Welsh valley, nature, landscape and farming were big influences on me. My work background is in sociology and community development work, though through years of work with Community Supported Agriculture models of farming, I was able to combine these two before embarking on creating a peasant bakery growing, milling and baking with heritage grains in Pembrokeshire, West Wales. I now live in Lithuania with my wife and two daughters. I offer support and advice to people and organisations engaged in community food production, heritage grains, milling and baking as well as teaching courses on these subjects. I am writing a Peasant Bakery Toolkit as a practical and philosophical resource for anyone interested in the cultivation, milling and baking of heritage grains in the global North. It is an invitation to anyone who feels called to become a peasant baker to be given the knowledge to be able to do it. The toolkit will cover most of what you need to know, from cultivation, to milling, to baking, infrastructure, economics, community, links to people and resources. Do get in touch if you want to know more: panisvita@protonmail.com

Rupert Dunn
Artisan baker

Bibliography

Bread baking

Bronwen, G., and Flinders, C. L., *Laurel's Kitchen Bread Book*, Random House, USA, 1984

Brown, E., *Tasajara Bread Book*, Shambhala Press, USA, 1995

Katzen, M., *The Moosewood Cookbook*, Ten Speed Press, USA, 1981

Whitley, A., *Bread Matters*, Fourth Estate, UK, 2006

Blessings

Cohen, W., *The Waldorf Book of Blessings*, Waldorf Publications, USA, 2022

Bread ovens

Denzer, K., *Build your Own Earth Oven*, Hand Print Press, OR, USA, 2001

Wing, D., and Scott, A., *The Bread Builders*, Chelsea Green Publishing, VT, USA, 1999

Education and child development

Druitt, A., Fynes-Clinton, C., and Rowling, M., *The Birthday Book*, Hawthorn Press, Stroud, UK, 2004

Goddard Blythe, S., *The Well Balanced Child*, Hawthorn Press, Stroud, UK, 2005

McAllen, A. E., *The Extra Lesson*, Rudolf Steiner Bookshop, London, UK, 1980

Martin, M., *Educating through Arts and Crafts*, Steiner Schools Fellowship Publications, Forest Row, UK, 1999

Oldfield, L., *Free to Learn*, Hawthorn Press, Stroud, UK, 2001

Steiner, R., *The Kingdom of Childhood*, Rudolf Steiner Press, London, UK, 1974

Nutrition

Cook, W. E., *Biodynamic Food and Cookbook*, Clairview Books, Forest Row, UK, 2006

Cook, W. E., *Foodwise*, Clairview Books, Forest Row, UK, 2003

Hauschka, R., *Nutrition – A Holistic Approach*, Sophia Books, Forest Row, UK, 2002

Schmidt, G., *The Dynamics of Nutrition*, Bio-Dynamic Literature, Rhode Island, USA, 1980

Coeliac disease

Green, P. H. R., and Jones, R., *Celiac Disease: A Hidden Epidemic*, Collins Press, USA, 2006

Korn, D., *Kids with Celiac Disease*, Woodbine House, USA, 2001

Songs, stories and poems

The Book of a Thousand Poems, Peter Bedrick Books, NY, 1983

Abbs, P., *Earth Songs*, Green Books, UK, 2002

Blood, P., *Rise Up Singing*, Sing Out Publication, PA, USA, 1992

Bruchac, J., *Native American Stories*, Fulcrum Publishing, Golden, Colorado, 1991

Jones, M., *Prayer and Graces*, Floris Books, Edinburgh, UK, 1980

Masters, B., *The Waldorf Song Book*, Floris Books, Edinburgh, UK, 1987

Price, C., *Let's Sing and Celebrate*, Songbird Press, Freeport, Maine, 2003

benShea, N., *Jacob the Baker*, Ballantine Books, NY, USA, 1989

Useful websites

Steiner/Waldorf education

www.awsna.org
www.steinerwaldorf.org.uk
www.waldorfanswers.org
www.waldorfeducation.org

Biodynamic and organic food

www.apricotcentre.co.uk
www.biodynamic.org.uk
www.biodynamics.com
www.hodmedods.co.uk
www.soilassociation.org
www.onlyorganic.org

Coeliac disease/Allergies/Sensitivites

www.home.allergicchild.com
www.celiac.org
www.celiac.com
www.coeliac.org.uk
www.aoecs.org/coeliac-disease/international-
coeliac-day/
www.food-info.net/uk/intol/gluten.htm

Author's website

To book a lively bread baking and /or bread oven building workshop, please consult my website which has detailed descriptions of all upcoming bread events for adults and children. This site includes many bread related resources and useful links. Come browse while the buns are in the oven.

www.www.handsfollowheart.com/warren/about/

Other books from Hawthorn Press

My Family and Other Allergies
Safe and scrumptious recipes for diverse diets
JULIE GRITTEN

Over 130 illustrated recipes and 20 chapters covering dietary issues such as diabetes, gluten and other intolerances, veganism, IBS and additives and how to work around them to cater for everyone at your table.

144pp; 246 x 189mm; paperback; ISBN: 978-1-912480-53-1

The Children's Forest
Stories & songs, wild food, crafts & celebrations, all year round
DAWN CASEY, ANNA RICHARDSON, HELEN D'ASCOLI

A rich and abundant treasury in celebration of the outdoors, this book encourages children's natural fascination with the forest and its inhabitants. An enchanting book where imagination, story and play bring alive the world of the forest. Full of games, facts, celebrations, craft activities, recipes, foraging, stories and Forest School skills, Ideal for ages 5-12 it will be enjoyed by all ages.

336pp; 250 x 200mm; paperback; ISBN: 978-1-907359-91-0

Creative Nature Play
NADEZHDA OSTRETSOVA

Learn how to make simple craft projects from natural objects, such as pine-cones and sheep's wool. Magically illustrated with crafts, stories, rhymes & games, suitable for children aged 5–8 years. *Creative Nature Play* connects children with nature, developing hand-eye co-ordination, dexterity and imagination with age-appropriate projects. Tips for teaching are included along with charming rhymes, anecdotes and stories to keep children playfully engaged.

64pp; 208 x 198mm; paperback; ISBN: 978-1-912480-84-5

A Year with Findus
Seasonal crafts and nature activities
SVEN NORDQVIST

Join Findus and Pettson and discover how much of what surrounds us can be reused and recycled. Beautifully brought to life by Sven's ingenious illustrations this book suggests crafts and activities using what nature has to offer. Learn how you can help animals and plants by collecting, fixing, crafting, building, exploring and baking. Fun, climate-friendly and affordable!

104pp; 240 x 160mm; hardback; ISBN: 978-1912480-89-0

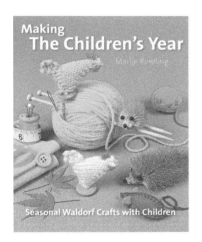

Making the Children's Year
Seasonal Waldorf Crafts with Children
MARIJE ROWLING

Drawing on the creative ethos of Steiner Waldorf education, this is a full-colour second edition of *The Children's Year*. Packed with all kinds of seasonal crafts, for beginners and experienced crafters, this book is a gift for parents seeking to make toys that will inspire children and provide an alternative to throwaway culture.

240pp; 250 x 200mm; paperback; ISBN 978-1-907359-69-9

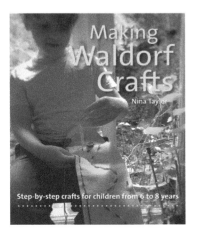

Making Waldorf Crafts
Step-by step crafts for children from 6 to 8 years
NINA TAYLOR

Practical craft projects suitable for children aged 6–8 years, classes 1 and 2 of Steiner-Waldorf school to follow on their own or with support. Techniques include spinning, knitting, sewing and weaving and the projects and techniques are accompanied by stories and anecdotes with a narrative that children won't be able to resist.

128pp: 250 X 200mm; paperback; ISBN: 978-1-912480-39-5

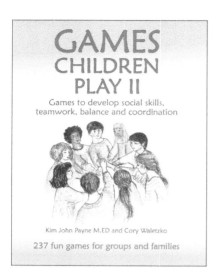

Games Children Play II
Games to develop social skills, teamwork, balance and coordination: 237 fun games for groups and families
KIM JOHN PAYNE AND CORY WALETZKO

This classic games book offers a standby resource for parents, teachers, forest school educators and play leaders. The games draw on worldwide Steiner-Waldorf creative education, where a 'child's work is their play.' Child growth is explored through a rich treasury of finger, clapping, beanbag, chasing, water, story and singing games.

264pp; 246 x 189mm; paperback; ISBN: 978-1-912480-52-4

Woodland Crafting
30 projects for children
PATRICK HARRISON

This book is guaranteed to get children out and about and enjoying nature. Through a series of stunning hand-drawn illustrations, *Woodland Crafting* provides the basic knowledge and skills to complete a range of both simple and more advanced craft projects.

96pp; 208 x 198mm; paperback; ISBN: 978-1-912480-83-8

Hawthorn Press

Ordering Books

Available from all good bookshops or direct from our website **www.hawthornpress.com**
UK distributor: Booksource; Tel 0845 370 0067; Email orders@booksource.net
USA distributor: Steinerbooks; Tel 703-661-1594; Email service@steinerbooks.org